THE PURPOSE OF PARLIAMENT

by Quintin Hogg

BLANDFORD PRESS

LONDON

Set and printed in Great Britain by
Tonbridge Printers Ltd., Peach Hall Works,
Tonbridge, Kent.
Published by Blandford Press Ltd.
16, West Central Street, London, W.C.1.

CONTENTS

Foreword

CHAPTER   PAGE

I. *The Purpose and Origin of Parliament* . 1

Secret of Britain's immunity from invasion and civil war. Parliamentary control and powers—forms of government—device for government by discussion—evolution of Parliamentary System—relationship between Crown and Parliament. Five periods of Parliament: (i) Medieval and Tudor monarchy; (ii) James I to Queen Anne; (iii) George I to Reform Act of 1832; (iv) Reform Bill to 1880; (v) Modern Parliament.

II. *Where Parliament Meets* . . . 7

Separate elements of King, Lords, and Commons. Establishment of permanent home and basic procedure. Mr. Churchill's speech on the new Chamber. Where Parliament met from thirteenth century onwards—four historic fires. Details of the building. Activity of Members.

III. *The King* 16

Powers of King—Norman era King central authority—conflict between King and aristocracy—powers vested in Parliament in Tudor era—eighteenth century Cabinet Government—gradual lessening of powers of kingship—functions of present sovereign.

IV. *The House of Lords* 22

The Chamber and places of Members. Procedure. History and origin. Composition of present House. Money Bills—no rights of amendment or rejection. Royal Prerogative to create peers. Observations on the Upper House and its survival.

V. *The House of Commons* 32

History and origin. Model Parliament—Edward I the originator—the franchise through the centuries. Salaries of Members.

iii

Contents

VI. *Members and Their Constituents* . . 40

The Commons numerically reviewed—details of constituencies and basis of electorates. Voting. Incomes and expenditures of Members. The Member and his constituency.

VII. *Privileges of Parliament* 47

Freedom of speech. Committal for contempt. Unfettered control of proceedings and Members— control of immediate surroundings of Westminster.

VIII. *The Powers of Parliament* . . . 52

Parliament legally omnipotent—consent of Parliament taken to be everyman's consent. Difference between Britain and other democratic countries. The weight of public opinion. Factors which prevent the British Constitution degenerating into a dictatorship.

IX. *The Cabinet* 59

Weekly meeting. Composition and functions of Cabinet—Privy Council—its origin. Appointments by the King. Salaries. Principal Ministers of Labour Government, 1945. Responsibility is collective. Authority of Cabinet. Administrative duties—Committee system—War Cabinet.

X. *The Parties* 74

Birth of parties. Early divisions of society—modern Party System following Reform Bill 1832. Party organization—origin of Labour Party—organization of Parties inside Parliament. Discipline— Whips. Party policies. The choice before electors— the floating vote.

XI. *His Majesty's Opposition* . . . 85

Almost peculiar to British Empire—its structure. Interplay between Government majority and the opposition's reasoning and objections. The power of the organized minority. Its functions—a responsible outlet for criticism—the organized expression of grievances. His Majesty's alternative government.

Contents

✓XII. *The Civil Service* 92

Civil Servants' gallery in House. Civil Service of modern and rapid growth. The administration and its influence. The relationship with the Ministers. The Civil Servant's job.

XIII. *The Press, Wireless, and Strangers' Gallery* 98

Importance of publicity. Keeping of journals from 1547. Press and Parliament—Reporters' gallery—Press correspondents—history of " Hansard." Broadcasting—Visitors' Gallery—Secret Sessions.

XIV. *What Happens at Elections* . . . 107

Selection and adoption of Candidates—"nursing" of Constituencies — nominations — duties of official Candidates—methods of conducting a campaign—election addresses and posters—broadcasting—Polling day activities—choosing a Candidate.

XV. *Basic Procedure* 117

Outlines of procedure evolved by end of medieval period. The Speaker. The Sergeant-at-Arms. Arrangement of places in Chamber. Speeches by Members—catching the Speaker's eye. Formal conventions. Procedure on taking the vote.

XVI. *Question Time* 124

History of its institution—increase in number—present quota—rules governing questions. Assistance given to Minister by Civil Service in replying—general procedure—written answers, and those by private notice. Raising the matter on the adjournment—the "business for next week" question.

✓XVII. *The Passing of a Bill* 130

Early petitioning of the King. A draft Act of Parliament. The parts of a Bill—Public, Private, and Hybrid Bills—Stages: First Reading, Second Reading, Committee, Report, Third Reading, House of Lords, Royal Assent.

Contents

XVIII. *The Humble Address, The Adjournment and on Resolutions* 140

Opening of Parliament—King's Speech—Government programme—the "Humble Address"—debate on Address. The Adjournment Debate. Resolutions as the vehicle for expression of opinion.

XIX. *Control of Executive* 144

Cabinet controlled by Commons—Commons controlled by Electorate—result a democracy. Instances of exercising of powers. Control of the purse and control of the sword. Debates on estimates, means of criticising Government. Emergency Powers Act.

XX. *To-day and To-morrow* 150

Growth of Parliament and attendant increase in volume of legislation—new burden of nationalizing major industries. Two main problems: (*a*) to reduce burden on time; (*b*) to retain principle of government by discussion—six suggestions: delegation to Cabinet, delegation to Local Authorities, delegation to Parliamentary Committees, reform Parliamentary Procedure, increased hours of sitting, World Parliament to discuss international problems. Extracts from Memorandum for Select Committee of Members' Salaries and Expenses.

XXI. *The Curtailment of Discussion* . . . 161

Details of weekly programme—pressure on Parliamentary time—curtailment of discussion by private Members. Equality of Members. Mutilation of rules of procedure—Gladstone's reforms—Closures—Delegated legislation—The 'Great Consumer'.

XXII. *Times and Seasons* 171

Summoning and dissolution of a Parliament—length of life — sessions — recesses — sittings — 11 o'clock Rule.

Contents

XXIII. *Comparisons and Queries* . . . 175

Conditions of existence and survival. Comparison with America—the Dominions. Political freedom and democracy—reasons for failure in other states. Parliamentary democracy based on Christian culture—capable of universal application.

XXIV. *A World Parliament?* 185

Speeches by Mr. Eden (Opposition) and Mr. Bevin (Labour Government) lead to conclusion that the next step may be World Parliament. Atomic bomb. Charter of United Nations Organization not sufficient—essentials of a free World Government—electoral basis, Executive, and Court. Spiritual conditions of success.

Index 193

Foreword

AS a system of government democracy has been known for rather more than two thousand five hundred years. In the fifth century B.C. the Athenian democracy coincided with one of the most remarkable efflorescences of art, literature, and culture ever known in the history of the human race. This early spring did not maintain its promise. Democracy brought disaster in its train and never really recovered its good name until to-day. Even now, its continued success, like that of other systems of government, cannot be regarded as certain.

With the Athenian experience particularly in mind, both Plato and Aristotle condemned democracy as a political system. Plato believed that democracy was not capable of survival, but on the contrary must always prove a temporary staging point between aristocracy and dictatorship.

So it has often proved both before and after Plato wrote. It happened in Rome where the half-hearted attempts of the popular party to substitute something more democratic for the system of aristocratic control by the senate was one of the main factors in the rise of Cæsarism. At a more rapid tempo, but with no less inevitability, the democratic phase of the French revolution was only an intermediate period between the absolutism of a traditional monarchy and that of the first of the modern dictators, and in more recent times the experience neither of Russia nor of Germany can be held to disprove the Platonic thesis. Representative institutions, giving a fixed and responsible character to democratic assemblies, clearly constitute an advance in technique over the assemblies of the City state. But representative institutions saved neither France, nor the Weimar Republic.

Nevertheless, one group of national constitutions seems to stand in marked and welcome contrast to the formidable list of failures. Great Britain, the United States of America, the British Dominions, the Scandinavian countries, Holland, Belgium and Switzerland all provide a sharp contrast to the history whether of Spanish republics, of Oriental tyrannies, of European feudal hierarchies, of modern revolutionary democracies, or the ancient city states of the Mediterranean. These countries have preserved the internal stability and vigour associated with an authoritative

A*

Executive without losing the freedom and tolerance of democratic and representative institutions. Is this good fortune or a matter of chance; or due to material and geographical factors unconnected with politics? Or are there other factors whose presence, or absence, makes for the success or failure of democratic institutions?

Our own constitution includes a powerful Executive, and an organized Opposition, both of which were lacking in France. Are these factors decisive? America has the former to a less degree, but not the latter; nevertheless, she possesses instead a system of checks and balances of her own which serve a similar purpose.

Even so, are constitutional forms and techniques in themselves sufficient magic to secure survival? Is it more than a coincidence that in each case where modern democracy has succeeded, it has been the child of a consciously Christian people? Is there a moral as well as a technical element in the success of democracy?

My own conclusion is that there is such an element; that conscious Christianity has been an important factor in the political stability of peoples in which successful democracy has been practised. Successful democracy depends neither upon mere good intentions, nor simply on political technique. If it meant no more than majority rule, to believe in democracy would be to indulge an insane preference for the tyranny of the many over the tyranny of the few. The truth is that the sovereign people, like any other sovereign, may be legally, but must not claim to be politically absolute. The rights of minorities, and individuals are as indispensable a factor in a democracy as the privileges of an anonymous majority. These rights can in the last resort be safeguarded only by the acceptance by the individual citizen of certain self-imposed moral disciplines. The clue to the nature of this standard of conduct can be found in the traditional theory of the natural law, a code as binding on a Christian democracy as upon a Christian prince. The spiritual and moral qualities and beliefs of a people are thus the ultimate safeguards of their liberty. Abandon these and tyranny or anarchy, or both, is the inevitable consequence. There is no security in any political theory that a happy state of affairs will be permanent. Such permanence depends on healthy constitutional technique and sound policies; if the former be destroyed or mutilated, or the latter abandoned, there can be no guarantee of the future. If history has a lesson in such a case it is that disaster is certain, perhaps the more overwhelming because it had been long delayed.

CHAPTER I

The Purpose and Origin of Parliament

WE are all apt to complain that there is a good deal wrong with our country and with this world. No doubt there is. But if we are driven to it we have to admit that Britain has been one of the happiest nations on the whole planet for quite a number of hundreds of years. To-day it is true that of all of the peoples in Europe, with the possible exception of Switzerland and Sweden, we are the only country enjoying something like a decent civilized and healthy standard of life. During the last two hundred years, alone of any country in Europe, we have remained immune from invasion and civil war. Every other nation of any size has during this time been devastated or occupied by hostile forces or has been the victim of violent explosions in consequence of civil disturbances. With the solitary exception of the Civil War in 1745, and of the more recent and still more melancholy history of violence in Ireland, we have been free from evils of both kinds.

What has been the secret of our good fortune? It is of course possible to subscribe to the theory that all foreigners enjoy a double dose of original sin and are being rewarded for their iniquities. But this theory, although agreeable, is hardly convincing.

It is possible also to explain the fact by reference to purely material considerations. We are an island and possess a magnificent natural defensive barrier, or we should assuredly have been overrun.

That our natural defences do in part explain our immunity from invasion will not be denied, but at the other end of the world Japan is also an island Empire more easily defensible than our own with a proud, abundant, intelligent and vigorous population. Yet she, too, came to disaster, even apart from this the fact that we live on an island can hardly explain our immunity from civil strife.

This book is written in the passionate belief that our safety and prosperity have not been purely a matter of chance; have not been simply due to an abundance of virtue on our part and cannot merely be explained as a matter of geography.

Politics may not be an exact science, but it is none the less an art of which the principles, however various in application, can be learned by a study of history and institutions.

Sound policy and an apt constitution have been at the bottom of Britain's immunity from defeat and civil war. This is the explanation frankly conceded over a space of more than two centuries by foreign observers—that our system of government · has been so nicely adjusted to the changing needs and temperaments of our own people that it is well nigh perfect, and that in so far as it lacks perfection it has the means within itself of achieving the necessary modifications.

Parliament is not the only feature of our constitution, and would not itself secure our survival if we pursued policies out of tune with the necessities of the time. But it is the central feature of our system of government, and this book is written in the hope that the institutions which have saved us in the past may not be permitted to suffer decay or collapse by the indifference or ignorance of the present time.

What is the purpose of Parliament? It is true that Parliament is the body which controls public finance, appoints and dismisses Governments, and under whose authority all our laws are passed, and that it is itself composed of members elected by the adult population of the country. But these are not ends in themselves. They are means to an end, attributes which Parliament possesses not for their own sake, but that Parliament may pursue its real object. The powers of Parliament are the marks of the successive struggles which had to be undergone before Parliament could achieve its purpose efficiently. The procedure of Parliament represents previously successful devices to put this purpose into operation. The underlying genius of Parliament lies in its power to realize this purpose in different ways through changing centuries.

Human government is either based on discussion or on force. This distinction is more fundamental than any classification based on differences of form, as, for instance, monarchy or republicanism, democracy or oligarchy. Each principle has its advocates. The advocates of force rightly say that as the march of an army is at the speed of its slowest unit, so in the realm of government administration by discussion can only proceed at the snail's pace enforced by the most stupid members of the community. Advocates of discussion may well reply with the fable of the hare and the tortoise. The dictatorships start off with a mighty rush. They are slowly but surely overtaken and passed by nations who rely on reason.

Of course all governments are to some extent a mixture of the two principles. No country is wholly governed by discussion. Human government is by its very nature compulsive and proceeds in the name of authority to coerce those who will not submit to law. Nor is any country wholly ruled by force. Human action is by its very nature voluntary and springs from reason by means of an act of will. But the essence of a despotism is that discussion is tolerated only when it is unavoidable; of free government, that discussion is a right and the willing compliance of all, a conscious objective.

Parliament is by its very definition an instrument of discussion. When I was in the Army, critics sometimes said to me that they could not understand what Members of Parliament were about. "They seem to do nothing but talk," was the complaint. My reply was, "That is why they are called a Parliament." The right to talk, to reason with Government before compulsion is brought to bear, is the foundation on which the whole of Parliamentary Government is built.

The object of Parliament is therefore not primarily efficiency in administration; indeed, in many ways it is obviously less efficient than a dictatorship. It is not even to achieve a logical or perfectly just system of laws, although over a period of centuries it is more likely to achieve this end than any other system of government.

Parliament is the device for government by discussion which Englishmen have developed through centuries in order that they may live in peace and unity with one another. I say Englishmen deliberately. Parliament was perfected in England, and transplanted across the seas by Englishmen. Other institutions we owe to the Irish, Scots and Welsh, and many of our greatest orators have been members of the Celtic peoples. But the institution itself is the specific contribution of God's Englishmen to the science of human government.

Although this is the purpose which Parliament has to achieve and by which it will ultimately be judged to be a success or failure, and although we must understand this purpose if we wish to follow its proceedings accurately or intelligently, we shall be surprised to find that this object is not avowed anywhere in any written constitution, nor shall we find the usages of Parliament conforming to any single logical plan. For the fact is that Parliament is not like a building designed and constructed by a single architect such as the Parthenon, St. Paul's Cathedral, or the Empire State Building. Parliament resembles rather an ancient family mansion which has been lived in continuously for a period of centuries, and has served the needs of those that have dwelt therein by constantly modifying and adding to its conveniences from generation to generation. In the centre there may be a Norman Keep—largely deserted now but giving its name to the whole and revered and venerated as the most ancient part of the building, and dating from the days when defence was the main object of architecture. Hard by is the Tudor wing—still serviceable and reflecting a period when first comfort began to take precedence over security. The Jacobean façade is the keynote of the whole, and the great staircase was the scene of a bloody encounter in the days of the Civil Wars. In Queen Anne's day they added a portico, and the great library dates from the Hanoverian period. The Victorian additions are commodious and well-built but somewhat ugly, while somewhere at the back scaffolding and a pile of bricks announce that something new is still being added to suit the needs of the present time. The whole has served the family well for generations of happy and vigorous life, but it baffles the planner to reduce its form to any single conception.

To those who live in it, it is a priceless possession not to be exchanged for anything more meretricious and unified. But those who are unfamiliar with its history are sometimes apt to lose themselves in its winding corridors and to be surprised and trapped by floors built at different times and on separate levels.

*   *   *   *   *

Parliament arose from the failure of the Norman Conquest to achieve biding peace and order in England. This was due to the weakness of the medieval monarchy. The revenues of the King were largely derived from the profits accruing from Crown lands and the extent to which custom enabled him to impose taxes or charge fees of quite a limited kind. So circumscribed was the ordinary revenues of a medieval monarch that we find Magna Carta and the early Parliaments solemnly recognizing special exceptions for taxes or charges to be specifically imposed, such as the knighting of the king's son or the marriage of his daughter. Such revenues did not suffice to support a strong executive Government in peace, much less to prosecute an effective war even with the assistance of knight service and the military tenure of land. The King was only *primus inter pares* amongst his barons, and barons and Church were themselves constantly at variance with one another and with the King. It was evident that without some new device the realm must disintegrate into a collection of independent powers. Parliament was the result of the resource and the genius of Edward I, pondering upon the disastrous weakness of John and Henry III and the constant necessity for war against the French and the Scots.

Edward I devised Parliament on the lines of a number of similar or analogous institutions which had always existed in Western European society.

Like other institutions of the time, the new body bore a close relationship to the medieval system of land tenure, but with the specific and new addition of the representative principle.

Thus from the start the relationship between Crown and Parliament was in one essential respect the same as that which obtains between the Government and Parliament to-day. The Crown was compelled by its own weakness to consult the realm before taking any large measure, and the work of Parliament consisted in voicing the opinion of the people in the presence and, if need be, to the despite of Government, and, on returning home, its Members had to declare the purpose of Government to those whom they represented.

The history of Parliament falls quite naturally into five periods:

The first includes the medieval period and the Tudor monarchy, and may be provisionally marked as coming to an end with the death of Queen Elizabeth. To this period must be assigned the basic structure of Parliament and its fundamental procedure.

The second period dates from the accession of James I to the death of Queen Anne. This period includes the long struggle with the Crown, and to it may be assigned the development of our financial procedure in Parliament as we now have it, and the present relationship between Parliament and the Crown as it has been recognized since the Act of Settlement.

The third period can be dated from the accession of George I to the passing of the Reform Act in 1832. To this period we owe the gradual development of Cabinet Government and the foundation of the party system within the House of Commons. We may call it the period of the unreformed Parliament.

The fourth period dates from the passing of the Reform Bill to the beginning of systematic Irish obstruction to the Liberal Government in 1880. This was the period during which the present relationship was established between Parliament and people, and to these years we must assign the rise of the great party organizations in the country.

The last period, that of the modern Parliament, may be said to date from Mr. Gladstone's reforms in Parliamentary procedure. During this time was erected the great modern administrative machine based on the Civil Service, and the almost complete control of the Parliamentary timetable by the Government of the day. We still live in this period, and we shall have to consider the difficulties and problems which it raises, and which we have still to solve.

CHAPTER II

Where Parliament Meets

BY the end of the reign of Queen Elizabeth, Parliament had established a permanent home, a permanent structure into the three separate elements of King, Lords and Commons, and a basic procedure which remains unaltered to the present day.

We must first consider this permanent home.

On October 28th, 1943, Mr. Winston Churchill moved in the House of Commons to set up a Committee for the rebuilding of the Chamber destroyed in 1941, without modification of its essential features. "We begin," he said, "by shaping our buildings. Afterwards our buildings shape us." Accordingly, the House voted by an overwhelming majority that their new Chamber was to be oblong and not horse-shoe shaped, was to be far too small to give seating accommodation to all its members at the same time, and was to be as uncomfortable as can be imagined, to be fitted with benches like the choir of a church and not with chairs like most other places of assembly in the world, still less with desks or separate seats for each Member.

This vote was supported, not on the practical ground that the Chamber which was to be rebuilt had to fit into the architectural plan of an existing structure, but on high constitutional doctrine. The oblong form of the Chamber is dictated by our unconquerable predilection for the two-party system, its small size and the absence of appointments by our immemorial habit of conducting important matters in an informal way.

"The semi-circular assembly," said the Prime Minister, "which appeals to the political theorists, enables every individual and every group to move round the centre adopting various shades of pink according as the weather changes. I am a convinced supporter of the Party system in preference to the group system. I have seen many earnest and ardent Parliaments destroyed by the group system. The Party system is much favoured by the oblong form of Chamber. It is easy for an individual to move through these insensible gradations from Left to Right, but the act of crossing the floor is one which requires serious consideration. I am well informed on

7

this matter, for I have accomplished that difficult process not only once but twice. Logic is a poor guide compared with custom; Logic, which has erected in so many countries semicircular assemblies which give every member not only a seat to sit on, but often a desk to write at, with a lid to bang, has proved fatal to Parliamentary Government as we know it here in its home and in the land of its birth."

He went on to deal with the limitation of size:

"If the House," he said, "is big enough to contain all its Members, nine-tenths of its debates will be conducted in the depressing atmosphere of an almost empty or half-empty Chamber. The essence of good House of Commons speaking is the conversational style, the facility for quick informal interruptions and interchanges. Harangues from a rostrum would be a bad substitute for the conversational style in which so much of our business is done. But the conversational style requires a fairly small space, and there should be on great occasions a sense of crowd and urgency."

This pronouncement was by far the most important of our constitutional system that has been made in years, and it is characteristic of British Parliamentary life that this acknowledged master of the Parliamentary art should have chosen as his occasion for making it a debate about the physical structure in which future discussions would be carried on. A review of our present-day constitutional arrangements begins therefore not unnaturally with a description of the central building in which Parliament assembles.

In the thirteenth century the Kings of England found the problems of the day too complex to be dealt with by the purely feudal polity which the Conqueror had founded. They therefore adopted the practice of holding a Council of their chief subjects. At first there may have been many different arrangements under which they met. We should not forget that Charles II was able to summon a Parliament at Oxford as late as March, 1681.

But by the middle of the fourteenth century Parliament sat regularly at Westminster in two distinct Houses as at present, the Lords spiritual and temporal sitting in one Chamber and the knights and burgesses of the Commons sitting elsewhere under the presidency of a Prolocutor or Speaker. The main body of the clergy, regularly summoned by proclamations, early ceased to observe the invitation and had their own dealings with the Crown through their Convocations until 1664.

The place at which the meetings were held was the Palace of Westminster, at the time and, until the acquisition of Whitehall by Henry VIII from Cardinal Wolsey, the actual residence of the King.

Until 1801, when they moved to the Court of Requests (a building on the site of the present statue of Richard Cœur de Lion), the Lords met in a building at the south end of the Palace. Until 1547 the Commons sat in the Chapter House of Westminster Abbey, which, in consequence, remains to this day under the control of the Office of Works instead of the Dean and Chapter. But in that year they moved to their historic home, St. Stephen's Chapel, in the Palace itself, the ground plan of which is exactly reproduced by the present St. Stephen's Hall in the existing building. It was the shape and size of St. Stephen's Chapel which gave the House of Commons its distinctive oblong shape, its inadequate accommodation, and the choir-like benches so much praised by Mr. Churchill, and to this day when the Speaker comes in to prayers he bows to the empty Chair which stands in front of the place formerly occupied by the altar.

The shape of the House of Lords has remained substantially the same from the earliest time. An extremely early picture depicting a Parliament of King Edward the First, with the King of Scotland sitting at his right hand, depicts the throne, the side benches, the cross-benches and the central square formed by the Woolsack, and the seats of the clerks and commissioners arranged in a manner very similar if not exactly the same as the present House of Lords since 1941, temporarily set up in the King's Robing Chamber.

The history of the buildings of Parliament is the history of four historic fires. The Chapel of St. Stephen, founded apparently by the king of that name, was burnt down in the reign of Edward the First, who rebuilt the chapel in the historic form which afterwards housed the Commons for 300 years. The second fire was in 1512, when the old royal residence was greatly damaged and thereafter completely abandoned by the King to Parliament. The third fire took place on October 16th, 1834, when the medieval Palace and all its ancillary buildings, apart from Westminster Hall, the Crypt Chapel and the Cloisters (now shamefully abused as the Members' Cloakroom) were almost totally destroyed. The fourth and latest fire was caused in May, 1941, by incendiary bombs from German aircraft during one of the greatest air raids on

9

London, and this has necessitated the present rebuilding of the House of Commons Chamber. Another parallel is also interesting. At present the House of Commons meets in the almost undamaged Chamber of the House of Lords. In this it is only following precedent. After the fire of 1834, while the present House was being rebuilt, the House of Lords of that time vacated the Court of Requests and lent the hospitality of its Chamber to the House of Commons, as its successor has done at the present day. Some of the earliest and best speeches of Gladstone and Disraeli were therefore made in the Chamber of the House of Lords.

The design of the present building is extremely complicated, not to say extravagant, and in proportion to the space covered the accommodation provided is both scanty and inconvenient.

The building lies along the bank of the Thames, which at Westminster Bridge is flowing almost from due south to due north. The central plan lies in the arrangement of the two Chambers situated on the first floor opposite to one another and connected by a series of passages and lobbies, with the throne at the south and the Speaker's Chair at the north of the axis so created, in such a way that with all the doors open the throne is visible from the Speaker's Chair. This line of corridors and lobbies is joined at its centre in the large Central Lobby by another axis coming in at right angles from the main public entrance at St. Stephen's porch. Parallel with the main axis are two lines of open courts surrounded by rooms and corridors: on the west, Star Chamber Court, Cloister Court, St. Stephen's Court, State Offices Court, and Chancellor's Court; on the east: Commons Court, Commons Inner Court, Peers' Inner Court, and Royal Court. East again lie the Speaker's Library, Commons Library, Members' Smoking-room, Members' Dining-room, and Peers' Library. Furthest to the east runs the Terrace along the riverside almost the whole length of the building, and famous in peace-time for its rich and agreeable teas of strawberries and cream.

West of Star Chamber Court and to the north of St. Stephen's porch is Westminster Hall, by far the oldest building of any in the Palace, being in the main of the time of William Rufus, alike the immemorial home of the English Common Law and the scene of many dramatic events in English history.

The fire of 1941 was the occasion of another remarkable coincidence. When a survey was made for suitable timber to repair the roof of Westminster Hall after the air raid, it was reported that the only oaks suitable for the purpose in the country were those on Sir George Courthope's estate in Sussex, and the records show that this very estate, Whiligh, provided the original timbers for the roof for William Rufus.

Within the complicated framework of these buildings are fitted countless apartments, a barber's shop, baths, a tea-room, a bar, several dining-rooms, a post-office, an office for the sale of Government publications, rooms for almost all the Ministers, a typing agency and, on the second floor a whole series of committee rooms. At the extreme north-east corner is the Speaker's residence, where he actually lives, with an equal house on the opposite side said to have been intended for the Lord Chancellor, but in fact never used by him in living memory. At the north-west corner is the Clock Tower and at the south-west the Victoria Tower by the Royal entrance. It had been the intention of Sir Charles Barry, the designer of the new building, to include the whole of New Palace Yard with lines of official offices surmounted by an additional tower, but by the time that this scheme was mooted, his backers had had enough and the plan was never adopted. The execution of his design had been thwarted throughout by continuous interference of interested and disinterested critics and he died a disappointed and disillusioned man.

It is obvious that the new repairs will not fundamentally alter the structure. The building is largely undamaged or repairable and, practically speaking, the only irreparable harm done is to the old House of Commons Chamber, which is completely burnt and neatly removed from the centre of the building to show the extraordinary Victorian ventilation and heating arrangements, the queer predecessors of modern air conditioning.

Now let me invite the reader to take a look at the Houses of Parliament about five o'clock on a sleepy afternoon in November, 1945.

We will begin by taking a look into the Chamber and see what is going on. The House is in Committee. The Speaker's Chair is therefore empty and the mace below the Table. In the Chair at the Table is Mr. Hubert Beaumont. The House is in the middle of a debate on the duties on motor vehicles.

Several well-known speakers have contributed to the debate. But the Government are taking a benevolently impartial attitude, having nothing to fear from the result. It is a substantial issue but not one of overriding importance. You will notice that there are not more than sixty or seventy members in the Chamber. However, I think we can leave them to talk it out. Come with me back into the Central Lobby and on to the Old Members' Lobby next to the place where the old House of Commons has been removed from the centre of the building.

Turn right, and go through the door at the end of the passage and you are in the library. If you walk with me through this room you will see almost as many Members as in the Chamber itself.

They are nearly all of them working—some of them are evidently preparing speeches. Mr. Molson (for instance), of High Peak, who likes to be accurate, is taking an old Hansard from a shelf. He is obviously verifying a reference from one of his opponent's speeches.

Others are dealing with letters. A fairly well-known member may get up to forty letters a day. You get no free secretarial services in the House of Commons, and a large proportion of members deal not merely with letters themselves, but actually write them. Well, there they are, dealing with them now. Often a letter from a constituent will necessitate writing two or three others to different people besides acknowledging the letter itself.

Now we will come out of the library and visit the tea-room, and the smoking-room, on our way up to the Committee floor. As it is tea time you will find them fairly full. I am not going to pretend they are very hard at work. But most of them are doing something fairly useful. We are elected to Parliament as members of a political party, and sometimes even of a section within the party. But most of us like to get to understand the other fellow's point of view, whether he belongs to a different wing of our own party or sits on the other side of the House. The smoking-room and the tea-room are the places where you often get to know people whose views interest you. Sometimes a question which transcends ordinary party differences crops up. Quite often discussions in the smoking-room have started quite important movements.

However, we have no more time for that at the moment. We take the lift opposite to the smoking-room and we are soon on the Committee Room floor. It is in the Committee rooms that the Standing Committees to which Bills are referred take place. These Committees are held in public, but some of the most important meetings are held in private.

Let us see what they are. We will go first to Committee Room No. 14, which holds the largest of the meetings. It is a large room arranged like the House of Commons itself, except that it has a sort of platform to seat a row of distinguished people as well as the Chairman. There is a picture behind representing the English fleet pursuing the Spaniards against Fowey, said to have been designed by the Prince Consort. The room is empty now, and in it are held the larger meetings such as the Scottish Grand Committee, the Standing Committees A, B, C and D which deal with Bills, the party meetings, the Conservative Members meeting every Wednesday afternoon and the Labour Members every morning at about half-past nine.

But many of the Committee meetings are not concerned with party politics. Recently Mr. Roy Harrod, the economist, addressed a meeting of Members of Parliament in the Grand Committee Room on the birth-rate; earlier the same session a joint committee meeting was held here to discuss the plight of the Jews, at which the Archbishop of Canterbury spoke. If we go now next door, past the Reporters' Room, we shall see a distinguished ex-soldier addressing a meeting of some forty or fifty M.P.s on the internal state of Europe. Further on a group, like the Committee which discusses air policy, or a larger Committee like the Tory Reform Committee, may be sitting.

The object of all these Committees, formal or informal, is to hammer out policy before presenting it in open debate in the House of Commons. This is done either by discussion between M.P.s themselves or by hearing distinguished experts. I will give an example of how this works in a moment.

But it is time we came down again to the main floor. If we turn to the right when we get to the bottom, and skirt the corridor at the side of the old Chamber, we come, first, to the Speaker's rooms, and then, if we turn left, we get to the rooms belonging to the Ministers.

It is here that Ministers do part of their work or receive deputations of Members. If we are lucky we shall see a deputation at one of the Minister's rooms just coming out now. No doubt there are others inside.

Now I hope the reader will agree that on the whole very few of the Members we have been seeing have been wasting their time, although three out of four have been outside the actual Chamber; neither those in the library, nor those in deputations, nor on the

Committee floor, nor even those in the smoking-rooms. Add to these the ones who are fulfilling some engagement in the country which they have got to do from time to time, if only to keep in touch with the electors, and I think you will begin to see why there were only sixty or seventy Members in the Chamber listening to Mr. ——'s amendment.

Before you go, I would like you to come back into the Central Lobby for a moment. Crowding round the policeman there are a whole group of people. They are "the public"; and the policeman is giving each a green card to fill up. Each green card represents a request to a Member in the House to leave whatever he happens to be doing and attend to the needs of the constituents. Sometimes these needs are important—sometimes less so. But at all events, poor Mr. Member of Parliament has to come out to see. You can see several Members talking to their visitors in the lobby. Now and again you will see one of the attendants going round with a sheaf of green cards and a few pink slips. The pink slips are telephone messages asking a Member to come out of the Chamber and ring somebody up.

A fairly good example of the way in which this sort of thing works might be given by the debate which is now going on on the floor of the Chamber.

This has been initiated by quite a small group of Members who wish to discuss the system of taxation on motor vehicles.

This is the first time that Members have thoroughly discussed this matter in public. But it would be wrong to assume from this that it was the first time that the matter has been discussed.

The Members concerned have in fact been dealing with the issue for some time. They have been getting letters which they have answered in the library, telephone slips and green cards; they have held private meetings on the Committee floor. They have interested other Members in the smoking-room. They have gone to other Committee meetings and raised the subject. They have visited Ministers in their private rooms in deputations or alone. They have written papers and circulars. They have collected information at Question-time. They have threatened to raise the matter on the Adjournment. They have put down two motions on the Order Paper and collected many signatures for each. They have then asked questions about it when "business" is discussed on Thursday.

Finally, they have seized the opportunity presented by the

Committee Stage of the Finance Bill to compel a discussion in which the matter will be finally decided.

It will be seen from this that weeks and months of patient work have gone into the preparation of the debate, or it would never have been held. Hours have gone in the preparation of the speeches. But all the House ever hears of it in the Chamber is one day's debate, and all the public ever hears is the shortened summary in the newspapers or in the wireless news.

While it is being held other people are, no doubt, making preparation to raise other subjects at a later time.

We shape the building; the building shapes us. Then we shape the building again to suit ourselves. When the new Chamber is finished a new chapter in the history of Parliament will be opened. I for one am not sorry that it will lead on continuously from the past.

CHAPTER III

The King

PARLIAMENT has three distinct parts—King, Lords, and Commons. Of these the King comes first, historically and constitutionally. If Parliament and Cabinet are the head and hands, the King is the heart of the British Constitution. He is the source of all legal energy, the only lawful origin of constitutional authority. The judges dispense justice in his name. The Cabinet hold their offices technically as his servants and advisers. Parliament is summoned to take up its duties by his proclamation. It is brought to an end by another Proclamation dissolving its existence. Its life is broken up into sessions created or prorogued under the Royal prerogative. Each Parliament, and each session of Parliament, is opened and closed by a personal visit from the King or by a Commission representing him under his Great Seal, and is made the occasion for a Speech put into his mouth by his Ministers explaining the policy of his Government and the circumstances in which Parliament is summoned, prorogued or dissolved. Before an Act becomes law it must receive his Assent expressed traditionally in Norman French, generally *Le Roy le veult*, or in a more complicated form for private or money Bills. The form of rejection, *Le Roy* (or *la reyne*) *s'avisera*, has not been heard since the days of Queen Anne, and may be considered defunct. Parliament is in form the Great Council of the Nation in which the King, advised by a Committee, the Cabinet Committee, of his Inner or Privy Council, exchanges views in public with his subjects. The meetings of the House of Commons are, in form, a withdrawal by the Lower Chamber to discuss amongst themselves the grievances they wish to put before the King through their Prolocutor or Speaker, or the answers they are to make to his requests through the same channel.

Parliament is complete in its traditional form when the King sits on his throne accompanied by his consort (on a slightly lower throne), placed in the presence of the House of Lords, but outside the bounds of their House, and of the faithful Commons assembled with their Speaker at the bar of the House of Lords and opposite the throne.

So much for legal theory. But the theory is more than a convenient fiction. The King represents the mystical element in the British Constitution without which, it seems, men can with difficulty be governed.

Men desire their laws and the system under which they are governed to be reasonable; but man does not live by bread, or by reason, alone, and the ultimate source of authority, reasonable as it must be, they desire to be clothed by something more majestic, sumptuous and inspiring than mere reason or naked force. The King is the lineal descendant of Egbert King of Wessex. His crown is called the Crown of the Confessor. His robes and the ceremonial of his Court represent the traditional emblems of majesty throughout the ages.

We who have not lived within a republic which owes its existence to some forcible, or possibly to some bloody, revolution can know nothing of the problems of conscience, excruciating and unanswerable, which torture good men under a Constitution which has no mystical claim to traditional obedience. Our King has risen above mere politics; his writ has become the guarantee of all that is legal and above board. There can be no Pétain, no Mussolini here so long as the King is true to his Coronation oath. The Crown is the symbol of our country as its wearer is an example to our fellow-countrymen.

This pre-eminence has been won at the cost of a complete and gradual self-sacrifice of the personal use of all political privileges and rights. The King reigns, but he has ceased to rule. His judges give justice. His Ministers make Orders in his name. His Parliament legislates. His forces prevail by land and sea. But none, except a select circle of intimate friends, is even permitted to know his real opinions on any of the controversial questions of the day. He selects only such advisers, makes only such laws as are agreeable to his Parliament, and appoints only such judges, bishops and commanders as these chosen advisers may select or approve.

The steps by which this has happened are matters of history. Britain has become a republic with a hereditary President clothed in the purple and prestige of majesty. America, whose Constitution is an earlier offshoot of the English tradition, in form a republic, is in fact a limited monarchy with an elective kingship guarded and hedged about with the checks and balances of a modified form of the British Constitution.

The steps by which the King reached his present position have been continous and regular; indeed, his full modern status may be said to have been crystallized only during the long and glorious reign of George V, and to have received full political recognition only during the abdication crisis of 1936.

The institution of monarchy is hidden in the mists of antiquity. The Kings of England were the descendants of the Kings of Wessex, who succeeded in prevailing over the other Kingdoms between Northumberland and Cornwall. In Saxon times their writ hardly ran to the North, but the victory at Hastings gave the Norman Government a strong central authority and based administration on the firm social foundation of a land-holding aristocracy which has only ceased to function in recent years. The history of the next centuries was very largely the history of a long and varying struggle between the authority and the aristocracy so created.

The advent of the Tudors brought this struggle to an end. All over Europe at this time great monarchies were breaking the power of great lords. This they succeeded in doing by two devices, control of finance, and the establishment of a standing army. The power of legislation was at that time subordinate; for in simple societies law is regarded as something not to be changed but only enforced, and administration is nine-tenths of Government.

On the continent of Europe this process led to the establishment of despotisms, like that of Louis XIV, under traditional kings, who only fell as the result of the series of revolutions beginning in 1789. Events in England, almost alone, took a different course.

This was due to two factors—that the Tudors used their Parliaments in order to establish their rule instead of ignoring them, and that the Stuarts were never able to persuade their Protestant and English subjects to trust them with the same instruments of power as had been given to their Continental brethren.

By 1702 this aspect of the struggle was over. Our Government was a limited, but not a constitutional monarchy. In a conflict between Parliament and Crown, Parliament prevailed, but it was still considered that for the most part the functions of monarch and Parliament were distinct and ought not to clash. The monarch still exercised such prerogatives as were left, and often created or overthrew Governments or Ministers.

The next step in the development of the British Constitution was the rise of Cabinet Government. The political accident which brought a dynasty of Germans to the throne of England left the conduct of administration to the interests which brought them there, and these rested on Parliament for their support.

This was considered an evil at the time. The functions of Government and law-making were, it was argued, distinct, and should be kept separate. The fathers of the American Constitution, abreast of the times as they thought, accepted this theory in framing their own model of Government. The American President is a limited monarch on the model of William III—elected and somewhat closely controlled, but still a monarch, who may differ from Congress in political complexion, and may pursue a different policy. His Cabinet are not members of Congress, and his mandate from the people distinct from that of the House of Representatives or Senate. The position is tolerable only because the spheres are legally defined, and the balance held by the Supreme Court.

In Britain this division of powers is not maintained. The royal powers of Government are exercised in their entirety (apart from the administration of Justice) by the King's Ministers, who are responsible to Members of Parliament. The laws passed by Parliament are passed (with few exceptions) only on the initiative of the King's Ministers. No conflict is possible because there is almost complete fusion between legislature and executive. This is the fruit, for good or ill, of the Hanoverian succession.

The personal intervention of the monarch ceased slowly. King George III revived the monarchy by bribing Parliament, and even Victoria, when a mere girl, overthrew Peel because she would not permit her Conservative Prime Minister to exclude Whigs from her entourage. Throughout her reign she acted with a good deal more independence than would be accepted to-day, and even King Edward VII committed breaches of what would to-day be considered constitutional etiquette. King George V's long reign stabilized and decided the modern position. The abdication crisis proved that a modern British Sovereign is so much the servant of his people that even his most intimate affairs are the concern of their representatives, his servants.

Nevertheless, it would be a mistake to underestimate the personal influence for good which a King may exercise in modern Britain.

"Our ancient hereditary monarchy," writes Mr. Amery, "is in a sense to-day essentially a symbol, the personal embodiment of the continuity and unity of our national and imperial life. But it is a symbol of immense and abiding potency. It stands as a continuous reminder to the Executive from top to bottom that its duty and responsibility are to the Crown; in other words, to the nation and to the Empire as a whole, and not to any party or section. Our ministers are the servants of the Crown. Our soldiers are the soldiers of the King and not of the Government of the day. It stands too for the strength and authority of government as such. We are proud of the fact that our system of government is parliamentary and democratic. But that does not mean that we are governed either by the electorate or even by Parliament. We are governed by the King in Parliament."

My own view is that this is an underestimate of the constitutional and personal responsibility of the Sovereign.

In the first place, the Sovereign remains the most important constitutional link with the Dominions. Canada, Australia, New Zealand, South Africa, all have their own Sovereign Parliaments. Each is free to legislate, to declare war, to make peace separately from its fellows or from the United Kingdom. The King, to quote constitutional theory, embodies in his person at least five monarchies, those of Great Britain, Canada, Australia, New Zealand, and South Africa. What the position of Eire may be is too delicate to answer on this side of St. George's Channel.

Secondly, the King is essentially the personal trustee, or guardian, of the Constitution. He cannot guarantee the people from the consequences of an act of folly at a general election. He cannot guarantee that his Ministers will not abuse their powers, or Parliament its unlimited sovereignty. But he can guarantee that no one but a duly appointed Minister will claim to exercise the prerogatives of Government, and nothing but a Parliament give laws in his name. No march on London could mimic the march on Rome unless the British Sovereign broke his coronation oath by entrusting the seals of office to Ministers who had not the backing of Parliament. The Courts would refuse to admit the validity of decrees issued by upstart Ministers or of any Reichstag summoned without the King's own Proclamation. If it is the Sovereign's duty to accept the advice of his Ministers in all things, it is also his duty to accept advice from no one else. There is reality behind the pageant.

Thirdly, there are two prerogatives which a modern king constantly exercises himself. It is he, suitably advised but really sovereign, who selects the order in which he sends for statesmen to assume the office of Prime Minister. Precedents there are in plenty, but none is quite decisive. The only limitation in his choice is the admitted necessity for the new Minister to obtain the support of a majority in the Commons. Let no one who has lived through a period in which a Baldwin was preferred to a Curzon, or a Churchill to a Halifax, minimise the importance of this selection.

Scarcely less important is the power of advice. In theory it is the Minister who advises the Sovereign, and this advice the Sovereign is bound to take. But although he must take it without offering a word of criticism in public, in private he can say exactly what he thinks of his Ministers to their face.

Lastly, we shall not appreciate the true flavour of the British monarchy if we do not admit that the functions of the Sovereign extend far beyond the purely political field.

The life of the Sovereign and his family plays in the life of the people that part which the great pagan festivals played in the life of the Roman populace. It is not primarily religious, although a royal marriage and a coronation ceremony are of more than temporal significance. It is the romanticizing of life itself, the gilding with all the pageantry and symbolism of royalty the life of the ordinary man. A royal birth becomes a festival of birth, royal children are depicted in nurseries and cottages as the very pattern of human childhood. A royal marriage is a national marriage festival, a coronation a national dedication. It is this fact that accounts for the immense popularity of the monarchy and the affectionate loyalty to the personality of the monarch. It is this also which gives rise to sharp sensitiveness to the Sovereign's observance of convention. For all the pomp and circumstance, the reigning monarch represents the enthronement of the ordinary man. He is one of us. He is no inspired musician, no profound scientist, no brilliant orator, no pretentious politician. He serves in the wars, but not really as a great Commander. In his person he symbolizes the virtues, the affections, the homeliness, even the humility of his ordinary subjects.

Other and prouder thrones have perished. George VI, by the Grace of God King, reigns over the hearts and affections of countless millions of his people.

CHAPTER IV

The House of Lords

IT is a foggy December morning in 1945. The House of Lords is in session in the small robing room prepared for their use when they gave up their more spacious Chamber to the Commons in 1941. It is a room about sixty feet by forty, and the Chamber itself is an artificially made inner portion carved out of the whole by two partition screens which leave corridors between them and the walls which serve for lobbies.

For the first time this Parliament, the Chamber is crowded and the galleries full and overflowing. The occasion is important, for their Lordships are debating the American Loan agreements and the terms of these documents are known to be repugnant to many of the Peers. At the head of the Chamber are two gilt chairs with the Royal Arms at the back. They are the only empty seats, but these are inviolable. They are placed on a series of three shallow steps covered with red carpet.

Lord Keynes is speaking from three rows back above the gangway on the left hand side. He is urging their Lordships to pass the loan. His voice is so quiet that it would be considered soft at a dinner table. But in this tense silence, and in this small Chamber, it is heard easily by a multitude. His points are cheered, and his jokes the subject of laughter as in the House of Commons. But cheers and laughter are infinitely more subdued, and hardly more than murmurs. It takes Lord Beaverbrook to stir their Lordships into something like disorder.

In this decorous assembly there are no effective rules of order. The Lord Chancellor wields no authority like the Speaker. Moreover, he pretends to no impartiality in the subject under discussion. Later he will rise to his feet, and will deliver a vigorous and lengthy speech in support of the loan.

Facing the Lord Chancellor is another peer sitting on another red sack. He has chosen that place for no better reason than that he is a little hard of hearing.

Further down, and in the centre, is the Table of the House with the wigged clerks sitting facing the throne and not, as in the Commons House, with their backs to the chair.

Ranged on the benches on either side are the Peers of the United Kingdom or of England, the Lords Spiritual, the representative Peers of Ireland and Scotland, and the Law Lords.

The Bishops sit on the bench immediately to the right of the Chancellor, the Ministers on the Front Bench further down and opposite the Table. On the left of the Chancellor, and above the gangway are the Liberal Peers. Immediately opposite the Ministers is the official opposition led by Lord Cranborne. In contrast to the two chairs, the steps of the throne are thick with reclining figures—Privy Councillors and Peers' heirs, while at the far end Members of the faithful Commons are milling in a closely-packed throng at the bar of the House.

Immediately in front of the throne a tall begowned and bewigged figure, the Lord Chancellor, sits in an attitude of the utmost despair upon the red-covered woolsack. Unlike the Speaker of the House of Commons, he sits on the same level as his Peers, and his despairing attitude is due to the fact that the woolsack affords a seat without arms, and with only a little raised back like the seat of a tramcar. Behind the little raised back the mace and his three-cornered hat are placed informally with the Great Purse (the symbol of the Chancellor's office), lying informally along the woolsack as an elderly gentleman might park his hat, umbrella and despatch case. When each Peer has finished another rises in a predetermined order. There is no bobbing crowd struggling to catch a Speaker's eye. If a noble Lord says something unparliamentary there are no means of suspending him or of expelling him from the House. The utmost that can be done is to read a standing order of the seventeenth century relating to violent language. The order is never read. There is no closure, no eleven o'clock rule, no guillotine and there is no sergeant-at-arms. The utmost sign of exasperation is that a noble Lord rises from the bench during a noble colleague's speech and moves quietly that "the noble Lord be no longer heard." I have no idea what happens if the motion is passed and the noble Lord continues to address the House. Nor have their Lordships. "You can't do that there 'ere." The rules of procedure are capable of every kind of abuse and are never read.

What is the composition? What are the powers, what is the history, and what is the future of this most interesting assembly?

If the institution of monarchy is the oldest, the House of Lords is the next oldest part of the Constitution.

No traditional monarchy is ever wholly absolute. Primitive Indo-European Societies were almost always governed by monarchs, but by monarchs advised and surrounded by a nobility based partly on birth, partly on prowess or wisdom, and partly on the King's caprice.

The history of constitutional government is very largely the story of a gradual shift of power from monarchs to an aristocracy, from an aristocracy to a middle class, from a middle class to a democracy. In ancient times, Persian, Greek, and Roman Kings were advised by a council whose Members did not entirely depend upon the King's will, and which developed into a formal deliberative assembly. The Roman historian Tacitus recognized a class of King's Companions who surround the Germanic chieftains and vied with them in military prowess. Our own Saxon Kings were advised by a Witan described by some as the ancestor of Parliament. But the truth is that an institution of this kind is common to all societies on the Indo-European model.

The House of Lords thus has origins far older than Parliament. The Norman kings, like their Saxon predecessors, held Great Councils of the realm, and these Great Councils consisted in those who in fact held the power—great princes of the Church, great Lords, judicial officers. In so far as the Norman monarchy had founded its new social order upon the feudal tenures of the land, the most common characteristic of those who attended upon the king in this way was the fact that they held land of the king direct in sufficient quantities to make it desirable that they should be summoned individually to the Council.

To the Great Councils of the Norman and Plantagenet Kings, then, were summoned by name the bulk of the great feudal landholders under the Crown, and the great Church dignitaries, abbots and bishops, who held large territories by virtue of their ecclesiastical office.

At first this summons was not a right but a privilege—but it was a privilege which it was not wise to withhold, and which very soon attached to the owners of certain estates in the form of a right. One of the earliest of these summonses is dated 1205 and addressed to the Bishop of Salisbury to attend a great Council to be held in London to discuss the message brought by envoys from Philip of France. By Magna Carta the King recognized it as a right of his people "to have the Common Council of the Kingdom" for the assessment of extraordinary aids and this was to include an individual summons "simply by letter" to archbishops, bishops, abbots, earls and greater barons. To this greater baronage, so described, the House of Lords may be said to trace its origin.

In other lands a different line of development has been pursued, with less fortunate results. In France and Germany nobility was a caste, a privilege of birth extending to all children, elder and younger, which marked them off from their less fortunate brethren.

Of such nobility English law has no knowledge; but as the law of the inheritance of great landed estates passed here by right of primogeniture to eldest sons, the peerage, that is the right to be summoned, became in this sense hereditary. The peerage, however, is not a castle of nobility in the continental sense. Younger sons are mere Commoners with no special privileges, and until they succeed to the title elder sons have no legal status apart from the customary right to listen to the debate of the House of Lords seated with the Privy Councillors on the steps of the throne, and, in the case of earldoms and above, the right to use a "courtesy title."

The peers—hereditary in this sense—continue to form the main portion of the House of Lords. Their titles do not now depend on the holding of a particular estate. The right to sit, once granted by the Crown by writ of Summons or by letters patent, cannot be withdrawn, but the King as the fountain of honour has an indefeasible prerogative to create an infinite number of new peers of any recognized rank. The hereditary peers are now divided into Dukes, Marquesses, Earls, Viscounts, and Barons, and number seven hundred and forty-eight,[1] composed of twenty-three Dukes (including three of the Blood Royal) twenty-seven Marquesses, one hundred and thirty-one Earls, eighty-nine Viscounts, and four hundred and eighty-eight Barons. By far the greater number of these are of very recent creation. Writing in 1938, Professor Laski observes:—

"Half the Membership of the House of Lords dates from the last fifty years. . . . In the eight years of his premiership Mr. Asquith recommended the creation of 108 peers, in six years Mr. Lloyd George created 115." The new Labour Government has already created eleven.

---

[1] The number of these is constantly varying by new creations and deaths without issue. The number is already different from that mentioned when the text was written.

These are the hereditary peers of England and of the United Kingdom. But before the two Acts of Union in 1707 and 1800, respectively, both Scotland and Ireland had separate peerages of their own. The survivors of these are not entitled as such to sit in the House of Lords, but to elect members of their order who sit there as their representatives.

The Scottish peers are entitled to elect sixteen representatives for every Parliament. The Irish representatives were elected for life. Since, following the Irish Treaty, no more elections of Irish peers have been or will be held, the eleven surviving Irish Representative peers are a somewhat melancholy and dwindling body. Those who have not been elected, like Lord Winterton, enjoy a happier, more carefree existence in the House of Commons or as private citizens.

The mitred abbots disappeared from the House of Lords at the Reformation. The bishops, however, remain, by custom twenty-six in number, including the two Archbishops, the Bishops of London, Durham, and Winchester, and the nineteen next most senior in order of seniority. These are the only representatives of the Church as such who now sit in Parliament, although from the earliest days the clergy have been regularly summoned by the Royal Proclamation to attend Parliament as a separate estate of the realm. For seven hundred years they neglected this summons. At first they taxed themselves in their own Convocations, but in 1664 the clergy submitted themselves to the ordinary taxes of the realm, and since that date have been a living contradiction of the phrase "no taxation without representation," since they are excluded from the House of Commons, although they exercise the vote.

These bodies account for the House of Lords, all but for six or seven members. A little select body of lawyers sits in the House of Lords, created barons by the Crown, but for life only. These are the "Law Lords" or "Lords of Appeal in Ordinary" created under Act of Parliament to enable the House of Lords to fulfil its judicial function as the Supreme Court of Appeal.

The membership of the House of Lords is therefore at present about eight hundred, composed of about 750 hereditary peers, sixteen representative Scottish peers, eleven surviving representative Irish peers, twenty-six bishops, and about six Lords of Appeal in Ordinary.

These eight hundred men collectively form the Upper House of Parliament, and are entitled individually to consider themselves Councillors of the King and to the privileges of Members of Parliament in the Upper House.

The powers of the House of Lords are limited, but not defined, by Act of Parliament. From the earliest days Lords and Commons debated separately, the Lords under the Chairmanship of the Lord Chancellor, and the Commons presided over by their own Speaker.

All legislation to be effective must pass each House, and each House requires that it pass three "readings" and a Committee Stage before they part with the measure.

At first sight, therefore, the House of Lords would appear to be the equal partner of the House of Commons under the King. This, however, is far from being the case. No doubt in the earliest days the Lords were the dominant partners, but this has ceased to be so from very early times.

As early as the reign of Richard II the formula for "money bills" tends to differ from that of ordinary legislation. For whereas ordinary legislation is enacted by the two Houses conjointly, in 1395, for the first time, it is recited that a grant has been "made" by the Commons and only "assented to" by the Lords.

At all events from Lancastrian days onwards, that is, from about 1400, the Commons began to claim primacy in matters of finance. Thus in 1407 King Henry IV assented to the principle that money grants were to be initiated in the House of Commons and not in the House of Lords, and when assented to by both Houses should be reported to the Crown by the Speaker of the House of Commons.

In the second place, from the early fourteenth century records, the Commons habitually interfered in what is called the "appropriation" of money. In other words, they insisted in money granted being earmarked for distinct purposes.

By the death of James I the granting of subsidies is primarily the function of the Commons as it is to-day, although as to-day the subsidies voted in what is now the Committee of Supply on Ways and Means require to be enacted in the form of a statute passing both Houses and assented to by the Crown.

By the reign of Charles II we find the Commons making even more considerable claims. Both in 1661 and 1671 they not merely asserted that the Lords could not initiate taxation, but they

27

insisted they could not even modify or amend proposals of this character, and in 1701 they used this principle which the Lords have tacitly accepted, in order to tack on to a money bill certain non-financial provisions which they did not desire the Lords to amend. From this moment onwards we may say that the Lords, although very powerful, became the junior partner in the business of Parliament, and preferred to exercise their influence to obtain control of the Commons rather than to exercise their rights and openly oppose the Lower House.

Under the Parliament Act 1911, passed as the result of the rejection by the Lords of the Budget of 1909, a Bill which is certified by the Speaker to be a Money Bill becomes law within one month whether or not the Lords consent to the Bill. Thus the Lords have now lost both their right of amendment and their right of rejection of Bills connected with the imposition of taxes or the expenditure of money, and retain only the right of public discussion of such measures.

This, of course, leaves untouched the great mass of legislation which is not mainly concerned with money.

Until 1911 the power of the Lords to amend or reject any measure of this kind with equal authority to the Commons was undoubted, although not unchallenged. If the Lords persisted in their difference with the Lower House, only the cumbrous device of a Conference between the representatives of both Houses (in which representatives of the Commons were usually twice as numerous as those of the Lords) could solve the difficulty. In practice the Lords seldom dared to challenge a new House of Commons like that which was elected to pass the Reform Bill in 1832, but theoretically the right was there.

In 1911 the right of rejection and amendment was reduced to a right of delay. After bitter controversy it was enacted that, if certain formalities were observed, an Act which passed the Commons in three successive sessions was to become law in spite of the House of Lords.

On paper this Act still leaves the House of Lords with a formidable legal power. A House of Lords which rejected the entire legislative programme of a modern Government could, in fact, prevent the work of Government being carried on at all, the more especially as it is now within the powers of the House of Lords under most Acts of Parliament to annul by resolution regulations enacted by a Minister. The House of Lords, although the junior partner, could, therefore, still prevent the business being carried on at all.

Why then does not a Labour Government immediately abolish the House of Lords, or the Conservative House of Lords immediately set about making the work of a Labour Government impossible?

The answer is, because the relations between the House of Commons and the House of Lords do not depend upon the Parliament Act at all.

The real balance of power lies now with the Commons, not in virtue of the powers acquired laboriously by custom, or by Act of Parliament, but by the Royal Prerogative which has existed all along, of creating as many peers as may be necessary to secure a Government majority. This prerogative would now be exercised on the advice of the Government of the day, which is representative of the House of Commons. With a Labour Administration, the House of Lords exists only on sufferance, because the Members of the House of Commons are limited, whereas those of the House of Lords are unlimited.

This device has only been resorted to once when the Tory Government of the day procured the creation of a number of new peers to carry the Treaty of Utrecht in 1713. Since then, both on the occasion of the Reform Bill (1832) and the Parliament Act (1911), the mere threat has been enough. Lord Asquith's biographers published, as a literary curiosity, the names of those whom he had it in mind to create. They almost make one wish that the Lords had rejected the Parliament Act.

It remains to be considered, however, whether it is really desirable to have a second Chamber whose powers are so illusory as those of the present House of Lords.

The Liberal framers of the Parliament Act thought it was not. In the preamble to the Act it was stated that:

"it is intended to substitute for the House of Lords as it exists a second Chamber constituted on a popular instead of a hereditary basis."

The Liberal majority which passed the Act has long since disappeared—but the House of Lords remains.

The Conservative Party has long been unanimous that Reform of the House of Lords is necessary. But Conservative majorities dominated the House of Commons for twenty years after the Parliament Act, and no effective attempt was made to reform the

House of Lords, which remains as hard to reform, yet as unconscionably long a-dying as the old Ottoman Empire.

No attempt was made to reform the House of Lords during the two minority Labour Governments of 1932 and 1929. No firm promise to "end or mend" the House of Lords was contained in the Labour election programme of 1945, and no sign has been given by the Labour Government now in office of a determined attempt to interfere either with its composition or its legal powers.

What is the explanation of this paradox? The truth is that while neither the composition nor the powers of the House of Lords is capable of any rational defence whatever, its actual working does very little harm even to a Labour Government, and is of very little assistance even to a Conservative Opposition.

To those who may by the accident of inheritance have peerages thrust upon them in the course of nature, the House of Lords is an intolerable nuisance. If the father of the author of this book were to die, Oxford City would be plunged into an unwanted by-election and put to an unnecessary expense and trouble, and its Member taken from the House of Commons which he loves, to support a peerage which he does not want in a state of life which he cannot afford. The heir to a peerage nowadays must put aside all major political ambition. He cannot be Prime Minister, Law Officer, or Chancellor of the Exchequer, and he is quite unlikely to be selected for most of the other posts of Government even though he might otherwise be the most suitable man for the job. He cannot abdicate, he must not resign, he may not even renounce his title in advance. He is the unwilling victim of an anachronistic survival from a social and political system which has long since passed away. It is surprising that no enterprising politician has voiced his grievance before.

In the meantime the House of Lords goes on. To quote from Professor Harold Laski: "If there is to be a second Chamber at all in a democratic State, the House of Lords, when a Conservative Government is in office, is perhaps as good a second Chamber as there is in the world. Its debates reach a high standard; it does not have to consider any temporary gusts of passion by which an electorate may be swept. It has time to discuss all kinds of issues which require ventilation, and can hardly hope for discussion in the overburdened House of Commons. Like important correspondence in *The Times*, it provides a useful sounding board.

It can raise large public questions which the Government does not yet believe to be ripe for legislation. It can scrutinize with leisured efficiency the Bills sent up to it from the House of Commons."

The next few years will probably prove that this indefensible institution is as valuable, or as little valuable, under a Labour Government as under a Conservative. The average attendance is not above fifty. The number of hereditary peers who have not taken the oath, about one hundred, and divisions are becoming increasingly rare.

Such a Chamber, although it may be a source of embarrassment to those whom the accident of birth reserves for its undesired privileges, at least disproves the view of the Abbé Sieyes that if a second Chamber agrees with the first it is superfluous, while if it disagrees it is obnoxious. Bagehot wrote of the House of Lords less convincingly:

"The order of nobility is of great use not only in what it creates but what it prevents. It prevents the rule of wealth, the religion of gold." If this be not true, and if Ramsay Muir's and Professor Laski's definition of the Upper House as the "Common Fortress of Wealth" be more accurate, it is at least a fortress of which the keys have long since been surrendered to democracy.

CHAPTER V

The House of Commons

THE Great Council of the King was never confined to the greater baronage. From the reign of Henry II onwards those who attended included all those who held land direct from the King. These were too numerous and often too humble to attract an individual summons by letter.

These, to quote Magna Carta, were 'summoned in general by Sheriffs and Bailiffs,' and were entitled to attend as of right together with the greater barons who were summoned by letter.

The revolutionary device which transformed this heterogeneous collection of tenants in chief into the Lower House of Parliament was the principle of representation by election. This is the most momentous step forward in constitutional procedure, and was complete at least by 1295, the year of the Model Parliament.

The idea of election is of course extremely old. Magistrates were elected in the cities of ancient Greece and Rome, as the President of the United States is in effect elected to-day. But like the President of the United States, they were elected to perform a given office and not to represent whole areas of a kingdom. The body in ancient times which 'represented' the Common people was the assembly of all the people, which all the people who were available were entitled to attend. Such assemblies were variable and inconstant in size and composition, and irresponsible, and extremely capricious in outlook. The arrival of the fleet in port, or an incursion of farmers from the country was quite enough in ancient Athens to alter the whole political complexion of the assembly.

A modern representative assembly is, however, of fixed size, composed of men and women whose names and opinions are known or ascertainable, and being elected for a period of time it has to observe a certain sense of responsibility and some degree of coherent policy. It also enables tracts of territory far greater than those comprised within the ancient City States to be ruled constitutionally in accordance with the wishes of the inhabitants. For this device the world has to thank Edward I.

Like most other new inventions, it was suggested by other institutions known at the time and appeared originally as an *ad hoc* experiment before it was adopted as normal constitutional practice. The notion of representation was not quite new, and was already linked up with the notion of taxation.

The feudal state was based on the theory that the King should live on his own resources, and that any additional monies should be presented to him by his subjects as a free gift. Thus until 1664 the clergy taxed themselves in Convocation and were not subject to the ordinary taxes of the land. No doubt in the early Councils the presence of great Lords individually summoned was particularly welcome as making it possible to receive their assent to proposals for the taxation of their lands. In the earliest assemblies Lords, Clergy, and Commons taxed themselves separately and at different rates.

From the reign of Henry II, a sort of representation had been prevalent in connection with taxation at the county assemblies called "Shire Moots," or, misleadingly to modern ears, the "County Courts." The reeve and four best men were to represent each township, twelve burgesses each borough. Four sworn knights were to nominate the recognitors at Henry's Grand Assize. Occasional examples of the principle of representation were soon found in the National assembly—at least five before the Parliaments of Edward I. In 1213 four men came from each township in the royal demesne. In 1254 two lawful and discreet knights were to come from each county. Representation of a number of knights, sometimes two or three, occurred on other occasions.

The revolutionary "Parliament" summoned by Simon de Montfort in 1265 not only represented the counties by two knights for each shire, but, perhaps for the first time, represented cities and boroughs by citizens and burgesses.

This is fundamental to the whole system of British representation. To this day county representation tends to be aristocratic—representation by squires or "minor barons"; the boroughs, on the other hand, when these have had democratic franchise, tend to both return people without aristocratic connections, and, whether this be so or not, are often willing to elect representatives living outside the boundaries of the borough. The divergence between the knights and burgesses was at first so great that they actually met separately, the knights associating with the Lords, leaving the burgesses in despised and insignificant isolation to represent the lower orders. If this arrangement had continued it is safe to say the British House of Commons could never have come into being.

The experimental assemblies of the reigns of John and Henry III were often called by the name of "colloquium"—or even 'Parliament"—which latter name applied originally and properly to the Council of Greater Barons sitting in its judicial capacity, the forerunners of the Appellate jurisdiction of the House of Lords.

It would be wrong, however, to ascribe the origins of Parliament to any other brain than that of Edward I, ruminating on the failures of the reigns of his two predecessors, the impoverishment of the realm, and the needs of his wars against Scots, Welsh and French. From 1275 onwards with increasing consistency he summoned representatives of all three estates, and from 1295 onwards, the year of the "Model Parliament," true Parliaments have assembled more or less on the classical model.

The structure devised by Edward I and his advisers has remained unchanged in its essential features until the present day. What is even more remarkable is that many, if not most, of the changes of recent years which go by the name of "reform" are, in reality, reversions to the earlier practice after centuries of corruption and abuse.

Thus the earliest franchise, perhaps because seats were not sought after, was amazingly democratic both in the counties and the towns. There is abundant evidence that all free men could vote. Voting was at the 'shiremoot' or 'county court,' and was by voice or show of hands. Only later, and in the case of dispute, did the party defeated on a show of hands, demand a "poll," which was, and remained until the middle of the nineteenth century, when the ballot was introduced, as open as voting in the House of Commons itself, and lasted over many days.

The early democratic franchise was later curtailed both in country and in town. In the country the vote was restricted in 1430 to the "forty shilling freeholders" of the county—a phrase, however, which was not strictly limited to holders of freehold land. Thus a chorister of Ely Cathedral, and the brewer, the baker, the bell-ringer, the gardener, the cook and the organ-blower of Westminster at one time either recorded or claimed to record votes in virtue of their offices. In the end there were eighty-five ways in which the county franchise could be claimed.

The democratic character of the franchise was however further vitiated by two other anomalies which drew their existence from the property qualification. These were the "faggot voter" and the absentee voter. The faggot voter was a person who had had a forty shilling freehold carved out of a larger freehold for the mere purpose of giving him a vote. The absentee voter was a resident in one county who owned a freehold in another solely for the purpose of acquiring a vote in that county. It will be readily seen that these two modifications of the county franchise weighed the balance in favour of the landed and moneyed interests and their nominees. All these developments had taken place before the accession of Charles I, and remained in existence either until the Reform Bill 1832 or later in the nineteenth century, when the property qualification was removed and voting by ballot introduced. Except for the introduction of voting by ballot, an adequate system of registration, and the principle of equality between the sexes, what we may be said to have achieved by the reform of the last century is a reversion to the purity of Edward I's Model Parliament.

The Borough franchise became even more wildly corrupt than that of the Counties. With all the defects in the electoral system, the knights of the Shire managed somehow to reflect public opinion. Borough and City members were to a far greater extent nominees of the Crown or of great interests.

Under medieval law boroughs could be created by Royal Charter without Parliamentary approval, and the Tudors began the practice of creating bogus Parliamentary boroughs simply in order to pack the House of Commons with their nominees. This had the effect of greatly increasing the number of boroughs represented in the House. Thus in 1295 the House of Commons included 200 burgesses representing about half the number of boroughs. By the reign of Edward III the number of burgesses had fallen to 180, but by the accession of Henry VIII there were 224, representing 111 cities and boroughs. Between the reigns of Henry VIII and Charles II no less than 180 more burgesses were added as the result of royal Charter.

This abuse was at first a blessing in disguise. Parliament had fallen into terribly low esteem at the end of the Wars of the Roses, and if the Tudors had chosen to ignore Parliament instead of using it deliberately as the chosen instrument of their rule we should never have enjoyed our freedom in later years. Yet the immediate consequences were thoroughly bad. Old boroughs had often declined in importance, and new boroughs were constantly created by the Crown not for their importance, but simply to produce safe seats until the reign of Charles II, when the House of Commons took the issue of writs into its own hands.

At first the change of control to the Commons was not beneficial, but simply transferred patronage from the Crown to the landed interests and more or less effectively prevented the creation of new boroughs, at the very moment when the industrial revolution was about to make it extremely urgent that numerous new boroughs should be created. Old boroughs became deserted (even where they had ever enjoyed a real importance) and became mere pieces of property in the hands of powerful lords. The result was that by 1832 the electoral map was one which could not possibly be supported. Representation in Parliament was concentrated in the South and West, and largely on the coast. Population was increasing rapidly in the Midlands and the North. Birmingham and Manchester, each with more than 100,000 people, were without Members, while in Cornwall there were forty-two seats for 300,000 people.[1] The number of "rotten" boroughs which sold themselves to the highest bidder and "pocket" boroughs which returned nominees of rich owners was very large.

The method of election to boroughs varied almost infinitely. Most democratic and nearest the pristine purity of Edward I was the "potwalloper" borough in which the right to vote depended on proof that the elector was the master of a fireplace at which he could cook his dinner. The potwalloper, however, entirely democratic in theory, failed to sustain in practice a high reputation for political integrity. In other cases the right to vote depended on the payment of local taxation; but in the main the borough franchise went with the possession of certain "burgage" properties, or was exercised by the municipal corporations or a closed body of "freemen of the borough." In my own constituency of Oxford the freemen fought the City Council and ultimately won the battle.

The numbers of the House of Commons, after an early increase, have remained surprisingly constant for three centuries. In the Model Parliament of 1295 the Members summoned were 274, that is 74 knights from 37 counties, plus the 200 citizens and burgesses.

---

[1] Keith, *op. cit.*, p. 21.

Apart from the increase in the boroughs, already noticed, Henry VIII added twenty-four for Wales (one for each of twelve counties and for each of twelve boroughs). The number of boroughs continued to increase slowly until the reign of Charles II, when the total number of Members of Parliament was 513.

A new category of Members was added by James I, who in 1603 enfranchised the two Universities of Oxford and Cambridge on account of the large number of local statutes affecting the colleges. On this precedent all the modern University franchises were created from time to time.

The Act of Union with Scotland added forty-five Members, and that with Ireland one hundred, but the number of English and Welsh Members remained until the Reform Bill at the exact figure of 513, which had been reached in the reign of Charles II. They were made up as follows:

40 English Counties	82 Members
12 Welsh Counties	12 ,,
24 Cities (including London, which then had four Members)	50 ,,
166 Boroughs	332 ,,
2 Universities	4 ,,
5 Single Member Boroughs . . .	5 ,,
8 Cinque Ports	16 ,,
12 Welsh Boroughs	12 ,,
	513 ,,

Add one hundred Members for Irish and forty-five for Scottish constituencies and you get a grand total in 1832 of 658 Members of the House of Commons. This figure of about 650 Members was retained after the Reform Bill until after the Irish treaty in 1922, when with the reduction in the Irish Members the number became 615. The present number has risen since 1945 to 640, owing to the division, as a temporary expedient, of some of the larger constituencies pending redistribution.

In one other aspect modern practice has returned to the custom of Edward I after a lapse into more corrupt usage lasting for centuries. This is the payment of Members. In the Middle Ages, as now, Members were paid for their services, knights at the rate of four shillings a day and burgesses at the rate of two shillings a day. These wages included travelling expenses, and were reckoned from the time they left their constituencies to the time when they returned home; journeys were calculated on the basis of twenty miles a day in winter, and thirty in summer—reasonably hard going.

The payment of these wages was always unpopular, and Members sometimes had to compound for a figure which was less than their due. Thus the Member for York in 1462 was only paid for twelve days instead of twenty as journey money. Less respectable still is the example of Canterbury, who in 1532 rewarded their Member with a new bonnet for sneaking home before Parliament was really over, and so saving his wages.

At first representation was a double burden—both on the Members selected and on the constituency which had to support them, and it was difficult to make either perform their obligations, and in consequence of the somewhat fragile morality of the times many corrupt bargains began to be made. But later a seat in Parliament came to be a much coveted honour. At first it was simply that Members would agree to serve for less than their due salary, and later to receive nothing at all. By the beginning of the seventeenth century wages were the exception rather than the rule, although we find reference to the payment of the Members for Devizes as late as 1641, and Kings Lynn in 1645, and as a final exception, the case of Hull, which paid wages to their Member, the poet Marvell, as late as 1678.

Later, however, Members began to pay for the more desirable seats. The earliest case of direct corruption of this kind was Hastings in 1640. But indirect payments and corrupt bargains of one sort or another were the rule until 1832, and have not in some measure ceased in our own day. I know of one pre-war Conservative Association which demanded a subscription of £3,000 a year from intending candidates if adopted, and figures of £500 a year for a "safe" seat were the rule rather than the exception. In the unreformed Parliament expenditure was even more staggering.

In still another aspect practice is gradually growing more wholesome. Between 1710 and 1858 so far from being paid, a Member was required to prove that he had an annual income from land amounting to £600 per year. This was designed to exclude what was considered the moneyed interest, that is, the interest which had funds but no land. In practice it succeeded in creating a vast number of subterfuges but in excluding no moneyed men, and very few poor ones—if they could otherwise become Members. Hardwick, Sheridan, Burke, Pope, and Wilkes all held their seats on more or less fictitious qualifications afforded by wealthy patrons, and Roebuck's father bought his son's qualification from Joseph Howe for a Reynolds' painting. One may wonder how far Mr. Disraeli was really qualified in his early days. The qualification was removed in 1858, and in 1911, for the first time in recent years, a salary was enacted of £400. This has now been raised to £600, and further increases are under consideration and may be expected.[1]

---

[1] Written before the publication of the Report of the Select Committee on Members' salaries and expenses.

CHAPTER VI

Members and Their Constituents

THE present House of Commons consists of six hundred and forty Members, each of them elected by the people, five hundred and seventeen from England, thirty-six from Wales, seventy-four from Scotland, and thirteen from Northern Ireland.

These six hundred and forty Members represent constituencies of three main types—counties, boroughs, and Universities. In addition to these it must be explained that the representation of the thirteen Northern Irish seats is based on the Federal principle, a different principle from that on which the other constituencies are elected.

Of the three main types of constituency outside Northern Ireland, there are two hundred and twenty-two English, twenty-four Welsh, and thirty-eight Scottish County Members, two hundred and sixteen English, eleven Welsh and thirty-three Scottish Borough Members. In addition, there are sixty-two Members for the County of London who are in effect Borough Members, although London ranks for some purposes as a County.

All the electorates in the constituencies except the Universities are based on the adult suffrage of the entire population of twenty-one years of age. Each man and each woman in the island becomes entitled to vote for the place or places of his or her residence on reaching the age of twenty-one. In addition, those who have businesses in any constituency may vote in that constituency (if they do not already do so) on a "business qualification." But no one may ever have two votes in the same constituency.

Where a single person has two or more votes in more constituencies than one, either by having more than one residence, or a residence and a business, or a business and a University qualification, or more than one University qualification, his voting is limited by the following rules:

(1) In a by-election he can vote for any constituency where he is qualified and registered.

(2) In a General Election he may use a maximum of two votes in two different constituencies, one, and not more than one, of which is a residence qualification. Thus he may vote in

his home constituency and in a business constituency or in his University constituency. He cannot vote in respect of two houses in which he resides, or two businesses, or two Universities, or a business and a University.

All the voting is done by ballot, that is, secretly, except in the University seats where it is done openly, by post, the voter signing his paper. The franchise is here limited to those with graduates' degrees, the one example in our constitution of the functional representation favoured by some modern continental systems. The Members returned would not in the main be likely to secure election by the ordinary franchise; the apparent anomaly in the Constitution tends to justify itself by the return of a race of men and women of high individual ability and normally independent of party ties.

In all the constituencies except the Universities the candidate with the largest number of votes is elected, notwithstanding that he has not an absolute majority. But in the University seats a system of proportional representation prevails which sometimes unseats a man who has received more first preference votes than his opponents.

Each of the county and borough constituencies returns one member to Parliament, except a few of the boroughs which still return two. The Universities, depending as they do on proportional representation, are not uniform. Some, like Queens University, Belfast, return one Member only; some are combined and share in two, like the combined English Universities. Some share three, like the Scottish Universities. Oxford, Cambridge and London are examples of individual Universities each returning two Members.

A constituency does not represent an exact number of voters or an exact area of ground, as conditions differ too greatly from place to place. There are three factors which generally govern or which ought generally to govern the size of a constituency.

(i) That a Member ought not to be asked to represent much more, and can reasonably be asked to represent not much less than a community containing fifty thousand electors.

(ii) That a Member ought not to be asked to represent an area in which he cannot reasonably travel round so as to visit all the different parts during an ordinary election campaign.

(iii) That territorial constituencies ought, so far as possible, to represent natural communities and not mere artificial boundaries.

(iv) That the balance of the United Kingdom as between its different parts should be more or less preserved.

In future the boundaries of constituencies will be constantly subject to regulation by a Boundary Commission set up under arrangements agreed during the war by the Coalition Government.

The Northern Irish seats are the only example of Federal representation in the United Kingdom. Under the original Home Rule Plan conceived in the Government of Ireland Act, 1920, the whole of Ireland was to be governed by two Irish Parliaments with additional Members in the Imperial Parliament. As a result of the Irish Treaty Southern Ireland was excluded from the scheme, but Northern Ireland continues to support a two-house legislature outside Belfast with limited powers and thirteen Members of the Imperial Parliament under the Government of Ireland Act, 1920.

Each Member of Parliament receives a salary of £600 a year from the time at which he takes his seat.[1] In addition he is entitled to free first-class railway travel between his constituency and Westminster, and between his registered home and Westminster.

Against the salary of £600, which is otherwise subject to tax, he can set off his expenses which may consist of secretarial assistance, office accommodation, salary of agent (if employed by the Member) extra living expenses either in his constituency or Westminster, travelling expenses, stationery, stamps, and telegrams and telephones. His expenses may not include the cost of his election or any charitable donations which his constituents can extract from him. A conscientious Member of Parliament can easily spend over £150 a year more than his salary in merely performing his duty as an M.P. A Member of Parliament loses his right to salary the moment he begins to draw salary as a Minister.

A recent author calculates that the most careful Member can hardly hope to do his work conscientiously and live a decent life with his wife and family at an annual income much under £1,000.

---

[1] At the moment of writing the report of a Select Committee which advocates an increase to £1,000 is under consideration.

Even a Member used to a working-class standard of life will require, he thinks, £350 a year in addition to his salary of £600, and if a higher standard is required the figure would be £1,500 or upwards.

In practice no Members, it may be assumed, live from their salaries. Labour Members are commonly in receipt of salaries from Trade Unions and Co-operative Societies. Other Members earn their living by journalism, the Bar, company directorships, or from other sources. The day when fortunes can be made from politics are happily over. The man who goes into Parliament may sometimes do so from unworthy motives—ambition, vanity or love of power; but greed is not a reason which can animate him reasonably. If this is his objective he is likely to be disappointed.

Indeed, he is likely to be disappointed unless he makes, and keeps his aims of the very highest. There are small thanks attached to being a Member of Parliament, and much work. Burke wrote to his constituents in 1774:—

"It ought to be the happiness and glory of a representative union, the closest correspondence, and the most unreserved communication with his constituents. Their wishes ought to have great weight with him, their opinion high respect, their business unremitted attention. It is his business to sacrifice his repose, his pleasures, his satisfactions to theirs, and above all, over, and in all cases, to prefer their interest to his own."

But Burke representing the Bristol of the eighteenth century can have had small conception of the pressure of business which weighs on a modern Member of Parliament representing a modern industrial or rural constituency of fifty thousand voters. Thirty letters a day pour into his letter box. Constant demands are made on his time, and even on his pocket. Five nights a week he must spend away from his home; two or three mornings are spent in Standing Committee. Lucky indeed he is if the House rises before the last train has left, and if during the recess he does not have to leave his own affairs in confusion to attend pressing business in his constituency. In return he can expect neither riches nor thanks. If he fails no man will speak well of him, if he succeeds his success will be attributed to questionable methods and low motives. When he is in, every pressure is brought to bear on him to prefer sectional to the national interests. If he refuses to listen to such suggestions all too often he is accused of want of responsiveness to the will of his constituents. If he complies, his compliance will be made the occasion for more unwarrantable demands.

Members of Parliament may not be dismissed by their constituents. Each new House of Commons is elected for the duration of the Parliament which may be five years or until dissolution. Until that time his constituents must put up with their Member as best they can until the next election, and even then if he does not care to stand they are denied the privilege of voting against him.

Theoretically, Members of Parliament cannot resign from their Membership; in practice they can do so by a legal fiction by which at their own request they are appointed to a fictitious "office of profit under the Crown"—the Stewardship of the Chiltern Hundreds of the Manor of Northstead—which vacates their seat.

Attempts have been made in the past to make Members of Parliament observe a certain standard of attendance; and in theory a Member of Parliament who desires to absent himself from the service of the House must still obtain leave of absence. In practice, however, no attempt to enforce attendance by anything except the Member's own conscience has ever succeeded. It is not practicable to say how much time each individual must spend in the House or travelling to improve his acquaintance with affairs, or keeping public engagements in the country or among his own constituents, or, since it is not thought desirable to make Parliament a whole-time employment, even in the management of his own affairs. Despite occasional scandals, the general standard of attention to duty is commendably high in all parties—and, as has been seen, the relatively low state of attendance in the Chamber on ordinary debates is no test of the way in which Members of Parliament do their job.

Writing of the position of a Member of Parliament some years ago Lord Snell observes:—

> "As a result of seven years' experience, I am convinced that the average Member of Parliament works at greater pressure and for longer hours than nine-tenths of those who elected him, and that if the factory worker, miner, or engineer had the same strain put upon him he would down tools within a month and demand better conditions of work."

Is a Member of Parliament bound to do what he is told by his constituents, or should he do what he thinks right on all occasions?

The answer is nearer the latter than the former. Although he is elected to represent a constituency, he is bound to prefer the interests of the country as a whole to any sectional interest, if they ultimately conflict. In the main, however, he will take the view that the interest of the country demands that the Member for Oxford should represent Oxford's interests among his fellow Members, even though these may sometimes think it right to overrule them.

Secondly, although he is elected, he is elected as a representative and not as a delegate. He is not under orders. The responsibility is his and he owes it to his conscience to do what he, and not his constituents think right. To preach any other doctrine would be to deprive debates in the House of any importance or weight whatever.

In the main, however, a conscientious man will be guided very largely by the opinion of his constituents; the fact that they hold an opinion very strongly will often influence his decision as to what he thinks it right to do, and, where he differs, he will only do so after careful reflexion and humble consideration of the defects of his own judgment.

The classical exposition of these sentiments is to be found in Burke's letter to his Bristol constituents in 1774, when he refused to be browbeaten into giving a pledge to obey their orders.

"His unbiassed opinion, his enlightened conscience, he ought not to sacrifice to you, to any man, or to any set of men living. These he does not derive from your pleasure; no, nor from the law and the Constitution. They are a trust from Providence, for the abuse of which he is deeply answerable. Your representative owes you, not his industry only, but his judgment; and he betrays, instead of serving you, if he sacrifices it to your opinion.

My worthy colleague says that his will ought to be subservient to yours. If that is all the thing is innocent. If government were a matter of will upon my side, yours, without question, ought to be superior. But government and legislation are matters of reason and judgment and not of inclination; and what sort of reason is that in which the determination precedes the discussion, in which one set of men deliberate, and another decide, and where those who form the conclusion are perhaps three hundred miles distant from those who hear the arguments.

To deliver an opinion is the right of all men; that of constituents is a weighty and respectable opinion, which a representative ought always to rejoice to hear and which he ought always most seriously to consider.

But authoritative instructions, mandates issued, which the Member is bound blindly and implicitly to obey to vote and to argue for, though contrary to the clearest conviction of his judgment and conscience—these are things which are utterly unknown to the laws of the land and which arise from a fundamental mistake of the whole order and tenor of our constitution.

Parliament is not a congress of ambassadors from different and hostile interests. Parliament is a deliberate assembly of one nation with one interest, that of the whole, where not local purposes or prejudices ought to guide but the general good resulting from the general reason of the whole. You choose a Member indeed. But when you have chosen him he is not a Member of Bristol, but a Member of Parliament."

CHAPTER VII

Privileges of Parliament

ALTHOUGH individual members do not now in practice receive many individual privileges as such, the House of Commons as a body enjoys extensive privileges over and above the functions of Government which it exercises.

The most important privilege is absolute freedom of speech. When Members are speaking in the House to their fellows they enjoy an absolute right of free speech, subject only to the rules of Order which they enforce themselves through the Speaker. A Member cannot be prosecuted for sedition, or sued for libel or slander in respect of anything he says during a debate in the House of Commons or publishes on its order paper.

This privilege, so obvious and axiomatic, was the subject for the most vital struggles for constitutional liberty in the past.

In early days the King's displeasure was the main source of danger for an outspoken Member. In 1397 the Commons adopted a Bill laid before them by one Haxey to reduce the charges of the Royal Household. The King demanded the name of the person who had introduced the Bill, and poor Mr. Haxey, M.P., was actually condemned to death for treason and would have been hanged, drawn and quartered if he had not been saved by Archbishop Arundell.[1] This, however, was an act of tyranny. Haxey took the opportunity of a new dynasty to get the judgment reversed as a breach of privilege in the first year of King Henry IV.

Apart from this case, in the main, freedom of speech in Parliament was generally recognized in the Middle Ages. The Tudors, who stabilized what was in a sense a modern European monarchy and the Stuarts, who wanted to maintain it, were much more definite in their assault on the principle.

Listen, for instance, to Queen Elizabeth's Lord Keeper[2] replying to the Speaker's customary petition for the recognition of privileges:—

---

[1] Anson's Law and Custom of the Constitution, fifth Edition, Chapter IV, p. 166.

[2] A Commoner, discharging the functions of Lord Chancellor.

"Privilege of speech is granted, but you must know what privilege you have—everyone what he listeth or what cometh into his brain to utter that. But your privilege is: Aye or No. Wherefore Mr. Speaker, Her Majesty's pleasure is, that if you perceive any idle heads that will not stick to hazard their own estates, which will meddle with reforming the Church, and transforming the Commonwealth, and do exhibit any Bills for such purpose, that you receive them not, until they be viewed and considered by those who it is fitter should consider of such things and can better judge them."

Under James I the battle for free speech began in earnest. As a result of Coke's strong speech against Spain the King ordered the Commons not to debate foreign policy, and when the Commons in reply protested their freedom of speech, the King tore the page out of the journal with his own hand—a fact still recorded on the following page by the Clerk of the House.

As might be expected, as the Civil War approached, the freedom of Parliament became one of the principal battlegrounds. In 1629 three Members were prosecuted and convicted for seditious speeches, and in 1641 the attempted impeachment of five Members of the House of Commons for High Treason was one of the events which precipitated the Civil War which ultimately cost Charles I his life. Under Charles II, the proceedings against the nine Members were solemnly reversed, and in the first year of William and Mary it was solemnly declared in the Bill of Rights, that "freedom of speech and debates and proceedings in Parliament ought not to be impeached or questioned in any Court or place in the land."

In the eighteenth century the only enemy of freedom was corruption. It was a common thing to deprive a Member of his commission in the Army (which he might hold without losing his seat) for his acts in Parliament. "We must silence this terrible Cornet of Dragoons," cried an angry Prime Minister of William Pitt the Elder, and as late as 1764 General Conway was dismissed from the Colonelcy of his regiment for opposing the Whig Minister of the day.

At the present time the sole disadvantage to being outspoken is the disapproval of official circles or not less commonly, a campaign of criticism in the Press.

The same absolute privilege now extends by Act of Parliament to the documents relating to its proceedings published by the Order of the House of Parliament.

This principle was established as the result of an exciting difference of opinion between the House and the Courts of Law which took place just over one hundred years ago in 1839 and 1840.

Hansard, the publisher of the original set of reports of Parliamentary proceedings, had by order of the House published an official report in which a book written by a Dr. Stockdale was twice referred to as "disgusting and obscene," and to his own disgust and surprise Hansard found himself the defendant in a libel action in which the plaintiff claimed £5,000 damages. The House of Commons supported Hansard, who pleaded privilege, and lost. Dr. Stockdale then ordered the Sheriff of Middlesex to levy execution on Hansard's press, which the Sheriff had to do. The House of Commons thereupon locked up the Sheriff in the Clocktower for contempt of the House, and the unlucky Sheriff in vain applied to the Courts for protection by habeas corpus.

By such strange and exciting episodes constitutional law is sometimes made.

This case well illustrates a second privilege the House of Commons enjoys if it cares to exercise it, the same power as a Court of Law—to imprison any subject for contempt of its proceedings. Even the Prince of Wales could be summoned to the bar of the House for contempt. For the same reason witnesses may be summoned and documents may be produced under compulsion before any of its Committees under the authority of the Speaker.

The right of punishment by committal is now rarely employed. Similar powers of punishment by admonition, reprimand or fine are also seldom used. But this is rather due to the unquestioned supremacy of the House in its own sphere rather than any relaxation of severity. Even in the present Parliament an unfortunate process server who sought to serve legal process within the precincts of the Palace was hauled before the Committee of Privileges, and managed to purge his contempt only by his evident ignorance of the great dangers he had run.

Thirdly, the House retains unfettered control both of its own proceedings and of its own Members. This extends even to the right of reporting proceedings, and to the exclusion of members of the public from debates. Originally the House insisted on all proceedings being in private—even behind locked doors for fear of interference from the Crown. Nowadays, secret sessions are not usually held except during a war for reasons of security, but individual Members still retain the right to "spy strangers," and a bewildered public can still be hustled out of the gallery if the House so decides.

This right extends to the exclusive powers of determining everything which goes on within the precincts of the House. Thus when Mr. Herbert, M.P., wished to draw attention to the licensing laws he sought to attract the attention of the King's Bench Division of the High Court to the fact that licensing laws were not observed in the Members' Smoking Room. The Courts decided that as the Houses of Parliament were technically a Royal Palace they had no jurisdiction to consider the matter.

Similarly, the House can claim complete control over its Members. A Member of Parliament cannot be suspended, punished or rebuked by his constituents.

The House of Commons possesses all these powers. In the eighteenth century it even claimed to expel a Member, John Wilkes, of whose behaviour the House disapproved, even though he was repeatedly re-elected by his constituents; and in the nineteenth century it exercised a series of extremely doubtful prerogatives in excluding Charles Bradlaugh from taking his seat, although he was willing to pronounce the words of the oath, on the ground that his known atheistical views rendered the ceremony an abuse. Even in 1945 a new Member, Dr. McIntyre, who presented himself to take the oath but was unwilling to provide himself with the usual sponsors was prevented for at least one day from taking his seat until the difficulty had been solved by his compliance. During the twenties of this century Members were commonly suspended for breaches of order, and they would be to-day but for the fact that the standard of decorum is noticeably higher and tempers better kept. The practice is that suspensions should be short, and should not lead to expulsion, and it says much for the dignity and authority of the House that they are almost invariably followed by an apology. But the legal powers of the House of Commons over its Members extend undoubtedly to suspension, imprisonment and expulsion—and possibly also to fine.

Other privileges have fallen into disuse. At the beginning of every Parliament in addition to the above, the King always graciously grants to his faithful Commons the right to have "the most favourable construction" placed on their actions. Individual

Members are theoretically free from arrest for debt, and might, in certain circumstances, refuse to give evidence in a civil cause. But these rights have fallen into disuse, and the only additional privilege which need be noticed is the control which the House of Commons claims to exercise over the immediate surroundings of Westminster under which traffic is held up for individual Members as they cross the street towards their place of duty, and public meetings are forbidden within a certain distance of the House.

CHAPTER VIII

The Powers of Parliament

WHAT can Parliament do? The answer, surprising as it may seem to American or Continental students of our Constitution is that legally Parliament is omnipotent. It can do anything. King, Lords and Commons proceeding in the time-honoured fashion by Act of Parliament can achieve any result which can be achieved by man-made laws.

"The most high and absolute power of the realm of England," writes Sir Thomas Smith,[1] "consisteth in the Parliament. For as in War, where the King himself in person, the nobility, the rest of the gentility and yeomanry are, is the force and power of England; so in peace and consultation where the prince is to give life and the last and highest commandment, the barony or nobility for the higher, the knights, esquires, gentlemen and commons for the lower part of the Commonwealth, the bishops for the clergy, be present to advertise consult and show what is good and necessary for the Commonwealth, and to consult together. . . . That is the Prince's and the whole realm's deed, whereof no man justly can complain, but must accommodate himself to find it good and obey it.

"That which is done by this consent is called firm, stable and sanctum, and is taken for law. The Parliament abrogateth old laws, maketh new, giveth order for things past and for things hereafter to be followed, changeth right and possessions of private men, legitimateth bastards, establisheth forms of religion, altereth weights and measures, giveth forms of succession to the crown, defineth of doubtful rights . . . . appointeth subsidies, tails taxes and impositions, giveth most free pardons and absolutions, restoreth in blood and name, as the highest court condemneth or absolveth them whom the prince will put to trial.[2] For every Englishman is intended to be present either in person or by procuration and attorney . . .

---

[1] Quoted by Redlich, "Proceedings of the House of Commons," i. 20.
[2] This reference to Act of Attainder, although still legally correct, is now obsolete.

from the prince . . . to the lowest person of England. And the consent of the Parliament is taken to be every man's consent."

Dicey's classical account of the matter begins with these words [1]:

"The sovereignty of Parliament is, from a legal point of view, the dominant characteristic of our political institutions. . . .

"The principle of Parliamentary sovereignty means nothing more or less than this, namely that Parliament . . . has under the English Constitution the right to make or unmake any law whatever, and further that no person or body is recognized by the law of England as having a right to override or set aside the legislation of Parliament."

He goes on to quote from Blackstone, the great legal author of the eighteenth century.

"The power and jurisdiction of Parliament," says Sir Edward Coke, "is so transcendant and absolute that it cannot be confined either for causes or persons within any bounds. . . . It can in short do everything that is not naturally impossible. . . . What Parliament doth no power on earth can undo."

I quote these passages at some length because this feature of the British Constitution is entirely foreign to those of most other democratic countries.

The American constitution, for example, clearly limits the rights which any one of its component parts may exercise, and establishes an authority, the Supreme Court, to see that they maintain these limits. If Congress or a State legislature pass Acts which exceed the function the body possesses, then the Supreme Court can declare the Act void; in particular, neither Congress nor a State legislature can by an Act modify the Constitution of the United States.

Most other democratic countries have legislatures which are to some extent limited, although not all have gone to the length of the United States in setting up a Court as a kind of ring-keeper in the matter.

---

[1] I ignore the criticisms of this passage by Dr. Wade in his Introduction to the Ninth Edition. Dr. Wade does not appreciate that the whole of Dicey's account is governed by the words in the first sentence "from a legal point of view," and his definition of what he means by law.

In Britain Parliament can do any legal act; it can legally put a subject to death, alter the succession of the Crown, enact the abdication of the King, postpone its own dissolution, modify the Constitution or alter the forms of religion, and the only possible legal limitation on its powers is that if it were to abolish itself completely it is uncertain whether a King by his proclamation might not summon a new Parliament which ignored the abolition.

This power of legal omnipotence is one of the most puissant factors in establishing the peculiar form of democracy in operation in England and known as Cabinet Government. As Parliament is legally as supreme as a Japanese Emperor, a body which dominates Parliament can exercise a power unknown elsewhere in extent. The power which whilst it does not dominate Parliament, at least exercises preponderating and usually decisive influence in Parliament is the Cabinet, and the Cabinet acquires this power by its control, through the Party system, of a Parliamentary majority in the House of Commons, combined with the right to create, through the use of the Royal prerogative, an unlimited number of Peers in the House of Lords, and the power to dissolve Parliament,[1] once, should it prove recalcitrant.

This, too, is wholly foreign to American or Continental practice. In America, Congress and the President are two separate powers of distinct composition, independent of one another, enjoying separate mandates from the people, not necessarily of identical political views, and in possession of separate but overlapping legal spheres of activity. On the Continent, democracies of the French model possess Parliaments presided over by Cabinets but with the balance of power reversed, for whereas in Britain the Cabinet normally exercises a control over the Parliament, abroad the Chamber of Deputies exercised a preponderating influence on the Cabinet, and whereas in Britain it is normally the Cabinet that brings about the dissolution of Parliament, in France it used to be the Chamber of Deputies that regularly overturned Cabinets.

The British working Constitution is dependent on a legally all-powerful Parliament elected by adult suffrage, but controlled through the machinery of party by Cabinet which are in fact the leaders of a single national party.

The only real factors which prevent the British Constitution degenerating into a dictatorship elected from time to time by a democratic constituency are the free speech and publicity of the

---

[1] See p. 68.

debates,[1] and the existence of an organized opposition in Parliament resting like the Cabinet on the support of a national party and in the country and competing with the Cabinet for the support of a floating vote.[2]

While the legal powers of Parliament are unlimited and the political power of the Cabinet enormous, it must be observed that they were obtained and are preserved by the observation of the most scrupulous limitations in practice.

It is not a coincidence that the forms of Parliament are in many respects unchanged since 1295. The authority and prestige of Parliament depend partly on the fact that its composition rests on a democratic suffrage, but almost equally on the fact that Parliaments summoned by Proclamation, composed of the same structural parts, meeting in the same geographical spot, passing laws by the same procedure have been going on for seven hundred years exercising the same powers with undisputed legal authority. There is a mystical element in the British Constitution which depends on an incredible conservatism of form which will none the less permit an almost indefinite flexibility of substance, and this mystical element of immemorial antiquity is as essential to its prestige and position as the solemnly indited written Constitution is essential to the peace and harmony of the United States of America. We smile at some of our usages, but we retain them. *"Ici on parle français,"* once shouted a Labour Member in the House of Lords when the Royal assent was being given in Norman French. But under a Labour Government a budget still becomes law because the sovereign through a Royal Commission under His Great Seal *"remercie ses bons sujets, accepte leur benevolences et ainsi le veult."*

Apart from the official opposition which we shall consider later, a more substantial limitation to the power of the Cabinet and Parliament lies in the independent organization of public opinion.

Constituencies as such are only organized by the parties. A town's meeting of constituents has no power to represent the will of the constituency, and a poll or referendum of Parliamentary electors is never held except for the purpose of the election of members to Parliament.

But quite apart from the political parties all the powerful interests in the State, trade unions, co-operatives, employers' societies, industries, professions, religions, societies, sports, even

---

[1] See p. 98 ff.   [2] See p. 85 ff.

local authorities, have immensely influential and wealthy organizations at their disposal ready to further their political or economic interests in Parliament and to threaten political action if their wishes are disregarded. Let no one who has witnessed the terrific rearguard action fought by the National Cyclists' Union against the imposition of rear lamps on bicycles, or that of some of the religious bodies against Sunday cinemas, ignore the importance of the sporting interest or the religious interests. It is probably untrue that any of these interests can impose their will on the Executive, and if they could it would be most unhealthy, but their cumulative influence against arbitrary or capricious use of executive authority can hardly be overestimated. It is literally true that no Education Act could pass Parliament without the most elaborate consultations with the local authorities, the teaching profession or the religious bodies. The parents, or the children, who are not organized as such, can, oddly enough, be more safely ignored.[1] It is not for nothing that when he wanted to destroy freedom Hitler destroyed first the political parties, but afterwards the trade unions, and voluntary societies, and did not stop even at the Rotarians, Boy Scouts, or sporting clubs. He was a bad man, yes, but not, as is commonly asserted, a fool. "Governments," says Dr. Wade,[2] "can no longer (*sic*) afford to disregard organized public opinion. The exercise of the law making power by Parliament is controlled almost exclusively by the Government of the day, placed in power by the possession of a majority in the Commons. But it is only used to coerce the subject after the subjects—through Chambers of Commerce, Federations of Industry, Trade Unions . . . have been consulted." Except that the example which Dr. Wade gives vastly underestimates the range and proliferation of effective bodies of organized opinion in a free society, this sentence fairly describes the position of Parliament at the present day.

A third and most vital limitation upon the rule of Parliament and Cabinet must now be mentioned. Parliament, Cabinet and people are all now, and in their due spheres sovereign, as sovereign as any king, or any dictator has ever been in law.

But there is a law to which sovereigns must submit. Henry de Bracton, Britain's oldest legal author, writes :

---

[1] This is sad; but the fact that the other bodies must be consulted is immensely salutary.

[2] Introduction to Dicey's "Law of the Constitution," 9th Edition, p. xlii.

"Est enim corona regis facere justitiam et judicium et tenere pacem sine quibus corona consistere non potest nec tenere." [1]

And one of the old judges speaking in Norman French said:

"La ley est la plus haute interitance que le roy ad. Car par la ley il meme et toutes ses sujets sont rules, et si la ley ne fuit nul roi et nul inheritance sera." [2]

No sovereign is, of course, bound by the law in the ordinary sense, at least in a modern State in which laws can be made at will and unmade. The maxim is: "The King can do no wrong," and this applies equally to an Act of Parliament or the Sovereign people.

But what these ancient lawyers had in mind was that no sovereign, prince or prime minister, dictator or electorate, monarch or Parliament, can disregard the "Law of Nature," that body of principles of right and wrong which constitute the covenants of the lease on the terms of which we hold this life.

What is the Law of Nature? No one has ever succeeded in defining it exactly, or with entire correctness; its application varies from case to case, from country to country, from century to century. To some, understanding of it is given more clearly than others; and we all, as individuals and as a race, are still learning its elementary principles.

But does it exist? Of course it does. It reappears again and again in different and varying forms:

"Naturam expellas furca tamen usque recurret."

Sometimes we see it contained in the judgment of a magistrate, sometimes in a philosophical work, sometimes in a Declaration of the Rights of Man, or a Great Charter, or Atlantic Charter, sometimes in a Tao, sometimes in an ancient code of Minos or Hamurrabi, sometimes in Twelve Tables, sometimes in Ten Commandments, and sometimes in a Golden Rule.

The point is that it is the same thing and the more perfectly we apprehend it the more certainly we see it to be the same throughout all ages. "Thy testimonies, O Lord, are sure."

"As God," says Blackstone in his Commentary on the English law, "created matter and endued it with a principle of mobility, established certain rules for the perpetual direction of that

---

[1] The crown of the King is to do justice and judgment and to maintain peace. Without this the crown cannot stand or hold together.

[2] This, a charming example of Anglo-Norman law French means, of course, "The Law is the highest inheritance which the King possesses. For by the Law the King himself is ruled as well as all his subjects, and if there were no Law, there would be no king and no inheritance."

motion; so when He created man and endued him with freewill to conduct himself in all parts of life, he laid down certain immutable laws whereby that freewill is in some degree regulated and restrained and gave him also the faculty of reason to discover the purport of those laws. . . . These are the eternal and immutable laws of good and evil to which the Creator himself in all his dispensations conforms. . . . Such among others are these principles: that we should live honestly, should hurt nobody and should render to everyone his due; to which three general precepts Justinian has reduced the whole doctrine of law.

"This law of nature being coeval with mankind and dictated by God Himself is, of course, superior in obligation to any other. It is binding all over the globe, in all countries and at all times. *No human laws are of any validity if contrary to this; and such of them as are valid derive all their force and all their authority mediately or immediately from this original.*"

The German maxim that right is what the Führer pleases is not merely wrong politically because dictatorship is an evil form of government; it is wrong ultimately because no sovereign—a democracy, a proletariat, or a Parliament, is entitled to do just what it pleases with others. Without the recognition of this, democracy is worse than a dictatorship because the rule of a large number of anonymous tyrants must be worse than that of a single known tyrant who can at least be assassinated. If any doubt this, let him read Thucydides' account of the evil side of Athenian democracy. *Corruptio optimi pessima.* Lucifer was an angel once.

This is the fundamental justification of Parliamentary government—but also its fundamental condition—the justification because, as Blackstone says, the Law of Nature is to be apprehended by reason, the condition because if Parliament ever abandons discussion, the instrument of reason, as the true guide, and substitutes some other test—a machine-made majority, a "doctrine of mandate" or the "popular will" or the "sovereign people" (*Das is Recht was dem Führer gefällt*) it will go the way of other tyrants, but not before it has involved the people in its ruin. For the sanction of the natural law is no court, nor any thunderbolt from heaven as our ancestors believed. Its sanction is the inevitable consequence of its disregard—the same sanction that attaches to the man who deliberately and habitually drives his car on the wrong side of the road. He will kill others, and he will himself in the end be killed.

CHAPTER IX

The Cabinet

IT is a drizzly morning in November. A small, uninterested crowd stands outside 10, Downing Street. Taxi-cabs and official cars draw up and deposit in ones and twos about twenty-five middle-aged or elderly men, not too well dressed, on the doorstep. Despatch cases, red boxes, and papers dribble unmethodically in and out. A single policeman surveys the scene with Olympian aloofness. The British Cabinet is holding its regular weekly meeting. Far remote are the pageantry and Oriental splendour of Government, the ermined magnificence of the Courts, the richness of the Lords, even the conventional dignity of the Speaker of the House of Commons. Yet here is the very seat of authority, the repository of power. This is the instrument of government, the brain and will of the State, the source of political energy and decision driving the policy of a great nation.

Let us follow the middle-aged gentlemen into the vestibule. A hall, a corridor, pegs for coats and hats, and finally a long eighteenth-century room, entered on its broad side, overlooking the Horse Guards and St. James Park. A long table, covered in blue cloth, clean sheets of paper and ink, ash trays. A curiously informal yet highly classical and well-bred kind of room, yet with a queer air of the country house about it. Two pillars mark the room into a sort of ante-chamber and a main portion. In just such a chamber an eighteenth-century aristocrat might read his papers before setting out for a day's sport.

The Prime Minister is in the Chair midway down the long side of the table with his back to the fireplace. Members of the Cabinet are seated round. A member of the Cabinet Secretariat has prepared the agenda and takes the Minutes.

Proceedings start. Discussion, even controversy, sways backwards and forwards. Ministers normally support with argument and repartee the interest and viewpoint of their particular department. Inside the Cabinet-room the convention of unanimity is non-existent. Occasionally genuine political differences between colleagues enlivens—almost embitters—the even flow of the controversy. In the end the Prime Minister sums up the discussion:

a decision is arrived at taking the sense of the meeting. It is unusual and it used to be claimed to be contrary to practice for a vote to be taken, or formal resolutions moved. Decisions are reached by the Cabinet of an Empire in the same method as those of a punchayat of village elders discussing public affairs beneath the banyan tree.

The British Cabinet is the prime instrument of modern government in this country, and its most characteristic feature.

Professor Berriedale Keith [1] thus summarizes an authoritative statement of the functions of the Cabinet given by the machinery of Government Committee, 1918. "They comprise (*a*) the final determination of the policy to be submitted to Parliament, (*b*) the supreme control of the national executive in accordance with the policy prescribed by Parliament, and (*c*) the continuous co-ordination and delimitation of the authorities of the several departments of state."

The functions of the Cabinet are, in fact, even more all-embracing than this summary might seem to imply. There are no real limits to what it may discuss and pronounce upon—indeed, the only safe generalization is that it should discuss and pronounce upon all matters considered of sufficient importance.

Professor Keith goes on to say:

"All matters of importance in the administrative sphere (including a course of departmental reorganization) . . . should be brought before the Cabinet as a matter of loyalty and the Cabinet has just grounds for dissatisfaction if this rule is ignored. This rule is equally binding on the Premier himself."

To this general rule there are certain conventional exceptions of varying degrees of importance. Appointments and honours are generally, but not always, left to the Prime Minister and his advisers. The prerogative of mercy with its exercise is normally left to the Home Secretary, although one may assume that in cases raising issues of sufficient political importance this exception may be waived. The Campbell case in 1924, which brought down the first Labour Government, confirms the view that the prosecution and discontinuance of the prosecution of criminal offences ought to be left to the unfettered discretion of the Attorney-General as part of the administration of justice, and, needless to say, the judicial functions of the Lord Chancellor are to be treated as entirely distinct from any executive functions he may possess

---

[1] "The British Cabinet System," p. 110.

as a Minister of the Crown. For somewhat different reasons it is not customary for a Chancellor of the Exchequer to disclose to his colleagues impending changes in taxation. In one recent case even the advance information given as a concession was the subject of a considerable scandal which terminated the public career of two well-known public men. To this we must add that urgent matters especially in the realm of Foreign Policy have sometimes to be dealt with without prior consultation with the Cabinet. In such cases, however, the Cabinet should be informed and consulted at the earliest possible moment.

In general, one can say that in peace the Cabinet is the instrument by which Britain is governed subject only to support of a House of Commons elected by the people.

At first sight the Cabinet would appear to be paralleled by many analogies abroad in other Parliamentary democracies, and in most dictatorships. Government by a Council of twenty or less, often called a Cabinet, is an instrument not confined to Parliamentary Governments, to democracies or even in its essential characteristics, to modern states. Japan had a Cabinet—so did Hitler, and all deliberate assemblies have had or have sought to create executive committees which prepared the agenda and gave some lead on policy.

Technically the British Cabinet is a Committee of Members of the Privy Council. Historically, it grew up as an inner circle of advisers selected from the Council by the King himself. Partial independence of the Crown was achieved at the Hanoverian succession when a German king learned to rely upon the advice of a Whig Prime Minister as to who should be summoned and who excluded from the inner circle of confidential advisers, whose deliberations he no longer attended owing alike to his inability to understand the language in which their proceedings were conducted and the intricacies of the policies which they debated.

But although Cabinet rank carries with it membership of the Privy Council, and exacts from those who attain it the oath of secrecy which is the mark of a Privy Councillor's office, the Cabinet itself is not in fact a Committee of the larger body, which never meets as a whole except for formal business, never appoints the Cabinet, and exercises no current political functions at all.

The modern British Cabinet, however, has characteristics of its own, peculiar to itself and not shared by comparable bodies which are not actually imitative of the British system.

From one point of view the Cabinet can be regarded as a joint committee of both Houses of Parliament. It is composed entirely of members of one House of Parliament or another. Very exceptionally a member is appointed who has no seat in either House; in such circumstances a seat in the Commons or a peerage is in practice found for him before very long. Although there is no law to compel this practice to be followed, the Cabinet is thus, in fact, a joint Committee of Members of both Houses. In this respect it differs from the American Cabinet. According to the theory of the American Constitution the functions of Government, executive, legislature and judiciary, are separated, and it would be as wrong for the President and his Cabinet to be members of the House of Representatives or the Senate as we should regard it as wrong for the King or his judges to seek election to Parliament.[1]

But although the Cabinet is entirely composed of Members of Parliament it is not appointed by Parliament any more than as a Committee of Privy Councillors: it is appointed by the King, and it does not correspond to various shades of Parliamentary opinion as do Select Committees or other bodies appointed by the Houses as a whole.

The Government is appointed by the King on the advice of the Prime Minister. The Prime Minister also selects such of the principal Ministers as he thinks fit to form the Cabinet. These Ministers always include such high officers of State as the Chancellor of the Exchequer and the principal Secretaries of State, but even these do not hold the position by virtue of their office. Some officials, like the Attorney-General, are not usually members of the Cabinet, but it is entirely for the Prime Minister to say whether this shall be so or not, and sometimes his confidence in a particular Minister is such that he becomes a member, although not normally holding an office carrying with it Cabinet rank.

The normal peacetime Cabinet is nowadays composed of about twenty members comprising the Prime Minister, the main Departmental Chiefs, the holders of certain high offices not associated with an administrative department such as the Lord President of the Council or the Lord Privy Seal, and such other Ministers as the Prime Minister may select.

---

[1] I understand that this is one of the rare conventions of the American Constitution. There seems to be nothing in the written document to enforce this aspect of the separation of Powers.

Although the "Cabinet" or its members as such are never referred to in the written Constitution of this country, that is, in Statutes, or recorded decisions, the Ministers of the Crown Act, 1937, reflects what was then thought to be the current practice when it provided that the following officials in addition to the Prime Minister (who receives £10,000 a year) should receive annual salaries of £5,000, and who may ordinarily be assumed to carry Cabinet rank together with their departmental responsibility (if any). The Ministers are (excluding the Prime Minister):—

The Chancellor of the Exchequer.
The Secretaries of State for Foreign Affairs, Home Affairs, the Dominions, the Colonies, for War and for Air.
The First Lord of the Admiralty.
The President of the Board of Trade.
The Ministers of Agriculture, Education, Health, Labour, Transport, and for the Co-ordination of Defence, and with the proviso that if not members of the Cabinet their salary is only £3,000.
The Lord President of the Council.
The Lord Privy Seal.
The Postmaster-General.
The First Commissioner of Works.
The Chancellor of the Duchy of Lancaster.

In addition to these officials the Lord Chancellor (whose salary is £10,000) is usually a member of the Cabinet.

Certain changes and additions have been made since the war. Some of these may be considered to have been permanent. These include several new Ministries, and a class of Minister who, though not with a seat in the Cabinet are considered of Cabinet rank.

The principal Ministers of the Labour Government of 1945 were:—

Prime Minister .. .. Rt. Hon. C. R. Attlee, C.H., M.P.
Lord President of the Council Rt. Hon. Herbert Morrison, M.P.
Secretary of State for Foreign Rt. Hon. Ernest Bevin, M.P.
  Affairs.
Lord Privy Seal .. .. Rt. Hon, A. Greenwood, C.H., M.P.
Chancellor of the Ex- Rt. Hon. Hugh Dalton, M.P.
  chequer.

President of the Board of Trade.	Rt. Hon. Sir Stafford Cripps, K.C., M.P.
First Lord of the Admiralty	Rt. Hon. A. V. Alexander, C.H., M.P.
Lord Chancellor	Rt. Hon. Lord Jowitt.
Secretary of State for the Home Department.	Rt. Hon. J. Chuter Ede, M.P.
Secretary of State for Dominion Affairs.	Rt. Hon. Viscount Addison.
Secretary of State for India, and Secretary of State for Burma.	Rt. Hon. Lord Pethick-Lawrence.
Secretary of State for the Colonies.	Rt. Hon. G. H. Hall, M.P.
Secretary of State for War ..	Rt. Hon. J. J. Lawson, M.P.
Secretary of State for Air ..	Rt. Hon. Viscount Stangate, D.S.O., D.F.C.
Secretary of State for Scotland.	Rt. Hon. J. Westwood, M.P.
Minister of Labour and National Service.	Rt. Hon. G. A. Isaacs, M.P.
Minister of Fuel and Power	Rt. Hon. Emanuel Shinwell, M.P.
Minister of Education ..	Rt. Hon. Ellen Wilkinson, M.P.
Minister of Health	Rt. Hon. Aneurin Bevan, M.P.
Minister of Agriculture and Fisheries.	Rt. Hon. T. Williams, M.P.

After the Cabinet come a series of Ministers some of whom are now treated as of Cabinet rank. The four Law Officers of the Crown (Attorney-General, Solicitor-General, Lord Advocate and Solicitor-General for Scotland), and a host of Junior Ministers called Under-Secretaries, Financial Secretaries, Parliamentary Secretaries, Civil Lords, or Junior Lords, the majority of whom serve in some department under one of the higher Ministers of the Crown. These lesser fry are in an unenviable position, since they are bound by the doctrine of collective responsibility for all acts of Government policy, but are below the level at which they are consulted in advance. Such offices carry with them considerable administrative responsibility, and the frequent duty of answering questions in the House of Commons but not the power of influencing general policy.

All members of the Cabinet are Ministers of the Crown, and all are members of the party or collection of parties in Office. In this the Cabinet differs from the Cabinets of old-fashioned monarchies, or from Committees of County Councils or other Executive Committees of Societies or other bodies. The old Cabinet Councils, for instance, presided over by William II or Queen Anne were not normally of one party persuasion. Indeed, it was considered a most important prerogative of monarchy to select the best advisers from whatever party they came. This left the ultimate responsibility for decision with the Crown and took it away from the Cabinet as a whole.

Select Committees of the House of Commons, or the various Committees of the different local authorities are nowadays selected on a different principle, that of reflecting party opinion within the larger body. This, too, is in direct contrast to the theory of the British Cabinet system. It is not Parliament that governs but the King's Ministers responsible to Parliament. This is our way of applying the doctrine of the Separation of Powers which led the Americans to exclude their Cabinet from Congress altogether.

The objects of both plans are the same: (i) to secure a clear-cut policy on controversial matters free from unnecessary compromise, and (ii) to fix full responsibility for this policy on a given body of men free from the possibility of evasion.

The theory which follows from these considerations of collective Cabinet responsibility is the cornerstone of the working British Constitution. Under it, a Minister must shoulder responsibility for all aspects of Government policy or resign. To some extent, of course, this theory is and is known to be, a pure fiction. Every Government of more than one person is, in a real sense, a Coalition. The publication of the reminiscences, diaries and personal papers of Ministers shows that debates in Cabinet are often as sharply divergent, even as acrimonious, as those on the floor of the House. But not a word of this must leak out in public. A Minister must accept responsibility for everything, or resign. It is no use the Minister of Agriculture saying, "I do not approve of the Navy Estimates." He may not be heard to say this and remain in office.

To quote Professor Keith again:

> "It is essential to the modern Cabinet system that responsibility should be collective. Matters are discussed in Cabinet and a decision taken. It then becomes binding on every member of the Cabinet, and of course on every Minister

outside the Cabinet. He must vote for the Government's view if a vote is taken in Parliament. He must if called upon defend the decision. He must not excuse himself on the ground that he was outvoted. If he does not consent to take responsibility he must resign."

And on the duty of secrecy he says:

"It is inherent in the position of Cabinet Ministers that they should maintain the confidential character of their proceedings. The rules of secrecy apply to Cabinet deliberations and to proceedings of Cabinet Ministers."

This rule is subject to only one exception. If a Minister resigns he obtains permission from the Crown to reveal sufficient material to give an adequate explanation in a personal statement as to the reason for his resignation. He is, however, expected to confine himself to the minimum necessary, and it is not customary for him to "cut and come again." One personal statement is considered sufficient and he would be refused permission to publish material containing secrets of the Cabinet Rooms prior to his resignation. The publication of the memoirs of distinguished statesmen and generals after the close of the last war made a temporary but important precedent of exception to the stringency of the rule.

It remains to be seen how far and in what direction the precedent is followed this time. That it will not be ordinarily extended to peacetime is to be devoutly hoped. One can pay too great a price in transmitting accurate historical knowledge to posterity.

Sometimes one is asked why Coalition Governments usually fail under the British Parliamentary system. It is not simply, as Disraeli observed, that "England does not love Coalitions." It is that a Coalition Government is by its very implication a denial of the fundamental principle on which Cabinet responsibility rests—a Cabinet able to preserve its secrets and sufficiently united in principle to maintain its absolute loyalty to Cabinet decisions. Coalition Governments cannot in time of peace preserve these characteristics. Ministers owe a divided loyalty—to their Ministerial colleagues in the Cabinet and to their party colleagues outside it, and this puts them in a position which becomes impossible. Either they break with their party, as happened to the Ministers in the Coalition in 1922, or they insist on the dissolution of the Coalition Government and break with their colleagues as happened in 1945. Continued Coalition in time of peace would inevitably involve either the destruction of old parties and the formation of new or else the disappearance of the form of Government which has been characteristic of this island since 1714.

The theory that they are party men representative of the dominant party in the House of Commons, but responsible to Parliament as a whole, Lords and Commons, Opposition and Government supporters alike, is the characteristic which differentiates the British system alike from all non-Parliamentary Governments, from Governments of the American type, and local Government Committees representative of all parties.

But surely, it will be asked, Cabinet Government is equally a characteristic of the French and other democratic constitutional systems?

The answer is that, as the American Constitution was modelled very largely on what the framers of it thought the British Constitution ought to have been like in 1770, so the Constitution of the Third Republic was to some extent modelled on what its framers believed that it should be like in 1870. But in each case the framers failed to mark some essential differences. The American Fathers tried to achieve an elected monarchy with a chief magistrate modelled on William III and a tenure of office for four years, and failed to observe that the real genius of the British Constitution at that time was dependent on the Prime Minister, and not his exuberant and unreliable sovereign. The Fathers of the French Constitution saw in the British Cabinet system an adequate model but strove successfully to subordinate the Cabinet, as they believed it should be, to the Chamber of Deputies, and ultimately to the people. They thereby fatally disturbed the balance of power in the Constitution and rendered it impossible for strong Governments to exist under the Third Republic. It was a mistake for which France in 1940 had to pay dearly.

A British Government has an immensely powerful weapon by which it can retain control of its supporters in the House of Commons, and the House of Commons as a result by custom pays deference to the Government of the day in three important ways.

The French Chamber of Deputies was elected for a definite period of years. Once elected it remained and could not be dissolved before that period was at an end.[1] A British Govern-

---

[1] It is interesting to see that in his draft Constitutional proposals, General de Gaulle devised some ingenious methods of curing this very fault.

ment, advising the Crown to exercise the same power of dissolution as Charles I employed, can appeal once from the House of Commons to the people which elected it. This means they can discipline their supporters with the threat of supplanting them in their constituencies with supporters of a more reliable type, and even their opponents with the threat of annihilation in the constituencies if the people do not approve their conduct.

This immense power can safely be used in a democracy only because it is based on the assumption that the Government is sufficiently popular to carry the electorate with it, and on the further convention, that if they are beaten the Government will not exercise the prerogative a second time, but will resign.

Thus it happens that though British Government depends on the Commons for support, it can still exercise the real authority of Government.

This authority is manifest in a variety of different ways. In the first place the party system has never degenerated in this country into a series of logrolling groups. In the second place, subject to certain vital limitations, the Government is permitted to control the entire time-table of the House of Commons. These two features of Parliament will be considered in their place.

In the meantime two other important consequences must be observed. Unlike the French Chamber of Deputies, the British House of Commons has never, since the rise of the British Cabinet system, attempted to rule the Government of the day by a series of Scrutinizing Committees of all parties. This was not always the case. During the struggle between Parliament and the Executive, such Committees were frequent. To-day only the Committee of Privileges, the Committee of Public Accounts, and the newly formed Committee to scrutinize delegated legislation exist as memorials to the older practice.

In the second place it is a fundamental characteristic of the British system that new taxes can only be proposed in the Commons House and only in that House by Ministers of the Crown. To quote from the Manual of Procedure:

> "The House does not receive a petition for any sum relating to the public service, or proceed upon any motion for a grant or charge upon the public revenue . . . except upon the recommendation of the Crown."

The standard work of Erskine May on Procedure puts it thus:

"The Crown demands money, the Commons grant it, and the Lords assent to the grant, but the Commons do not vote money unless it be required by the Crown; nor do they propose or augment taxes unless such taxation be necessary as declared by the Crown through its constitutional advisers."

In Professor Keith's words:

"One of the fundamental principles which renders the operation of Cabinet Government in Britain different from its operation in France is purely conventional—the rule that the Commons will deal with financial proposals only on the initiative of the Ministry with which there rests the framing of the Budget, the determination of expenditure and the devising of taxation. . . . The adoption of the same rule necessarily accompanied the creation of Cabinet Government in the British Colonies."

This rule is another illustration of the extent to which the Executive is stronger in Britain than in some other democracies. It dates, of course, from the time when the Commons regarded its main function as the prevention of unauthorized imposts. In modern days it is one of the many ways in which a government retains the initiative in matters of policy and legislation.

The formal meeting of the Cabinet is, of course, only a small part of the real work done by that body. It is the portion of the iceberg which emerges above the surface. A vast amount of administrative and preparatory work has to be done in order to make the official meetings possible and fruitful. This preparatory work consists partly in the circulation of Cabinet papers and Foreign Office telegrams for the purpose of keeping Ministers, and certain other high officials, informed of what is going on in other departments or in foreign countries, and partly in the elaborate system of Committees, Cabinet, Ministerial, and Official radiating from the Cabinet, preparing papers for its discussion, and smoothing out differences of policy.

Every day messengers can be seen carrying to Cabinet Ministers, wherever they happen to be, red or green boxes which contain the papers circulated for them to read. The boxes open with keys of a separate pattern which the Ministers carry on their persons. If one key is lost or missing a whole new issue of keys of that particular type has to be prepared and issued. The keys of each type of box are interchangeable with one another.

The mass of papers circulated is so large that if a Minister set himself to read them conscientiously it would take hours of his time every day to enable him to do so. The result is that confusion very often occurs from the mere quantity to be digested. Professor Keith records an instance dating from a period at which the quantity circulated was certainly not greater than it is now, when Lord Birkenhead bitterly reproached Lord Curzon for failing to circulate a despatch which he had not merely received but actually read.

No account of Cabinet Government would be complete without reference to the Committee system which radiates from it.

In a modern state, administration has become so far reaching and complicated that the most careful preparatory work has to be done before affairs are in a condition to be decided by the Cabinet.

Where the work is confined to the administration of a single department, this preparatory work is carried out under the arrangements of the Minister responsible for it. Preliminary investigations are made, meetings of experts are held on questions at issue, further meetings under the Presidency of the Minister and ultimately a paper for submission to the Cabinet prepared bearing the Minister's initials.

More usually, questions however apparently simple in fact, involve decisions by more than one department. This is a matter which is the constant alarm and despair of the general public who complain with bitterness and not without reason that they are being bandied about like a shuttlecock between department and department.

In reality this is the price we pay for having a complex system of administration. Matters apparently simple do involve more than one department and the public are usually the first to complain when policy in different departments is not in line. Housing does involve questions of local government, of labour, of town planning, of health, and often of agriculture, and while it is the business of Government not to confuse the individual with a welter of authorities each speaking with a separate voice, within its own organization, Committees involving very large numbers of separate interests are an indispensable instrument of policy.

Sometimes these Committees are instruments of administration like the Joint Air Priorities Board. Sometimes they meet irregularly for the purpose of maintaining a coherent policy on parallel matters like the Committee on Service Pay and Allowances. Sometimes they are convened to consider specific changes of policy on the implications of a particular project.

The less important Committees are purely official, but as they rise in weight and authority they become "Ministerial" Committees, composed mainly and wholly of officials but presided over by a Junior Minister, or even a Minister of Cabinet rank.

More important still are the Cabinet, or War Cabinet Committees which meet to discuss matters of the highest policy, and which are normally limited to Ministers of the highest rank.

THE WAR CABINET

The normal system of Cabinet Government may be said to break down under the strain of modern war. To quote Professor Keith:

> "Palpably in wartime, the Cabinet system has to be modified in some degree so as to secure the existence of a body which is in a position to take swift decisions without fear of their being disturbed."

In the two great wars of modern time the ordinary rule of the Cabinet has been superseded by a more flexible, and at the same time less definite and more arbitrary rule by a smaller Committee of great men known as the "War Cabinet."

The size and nature of this War Cabinet has, however, differed between the two wars. In World War I, the "War Cabinet" system was the creation of Mr. Lloyd George when he superseded Mr. Asquith as Prime Minister.

This War Cabinet superseded an earlier, and most inefficient body, the "War Council," which in turn had sprung indirectly from the Committee of Imperial Defence.

Lloyd George's War Cabinet was always extremely small and composed in the main of Ministers without Portfolio, free from direct departmental responsibility.

At the conclusion of the War in November, 1918, the War Cabinet consisted of:

(1) The Prime Minister .. .. .. Mr. Lloyd George.
(2) Lord President of the Council .. Lord Curzon.
(3) The Chancellor of the Exchequer .. Mr. Bonar Law.
(4), (5), (6), Ministers without Portfolio .. Mr. George Barnes.
General Smuts.
Mr. A. Chamberlain.

Mr. Neville Chamberlain began World War No. 2 with a War Cabinet which by contrast consisted almost entirely of Departmental Chiefs and was considerably larger in size.

This War Cabinet consisted of nine members in September, 1939, made up of the Prime Minister, Chancellor of the Exchequer, Secretary of State for Foreign Affairs, the three Service Ministers, the Lord Privy Seal, and one Minister without Portfolio.

Mr. Churchill in 1940 reverted to the earlier model, but his later War Cabinets partook of a mixed character, including more departmental chiefs and increasing slightly in size.

He began with five members composed of the Prime Minister, Mr. Neville Chamberlain (Lord President), Mr. Attlee, Lord Halifax (Foreign Secretary), and Lord Hankey.

But by the end of the War, Mr. Churchill's War Cabinet had risen to eight members of whom the majority had important departments at their command.

At the beginning of the 1944 session these were:

The Prime Minister.
The Deputy Prime Minister.
The Secretary of State for Foreign Affairs.
The Chancellor of the Exchequer.
The Minister of Labour.
The Minister of Production.
The Secretary of State for Home Affairs.
The Minister of Reconstruction.

It is plain, however, from the vagaries which the membership of the War Cabinet pursued during the war that membership of the War Cabinet depended more directly upon the Prime Minister's favour than upon the office which the Statesman happened to hold.

Thus the Minister of Aircraft Production (Lord Beaverbrook) was long a member. Sir John Anderson became a member as Lord President, and retained his seat as Chancellor of the Exchequer; while after Sir Kingsley Wood dropped out of the War Cabinet there was a considerable period during which the office of Chancellor was not held by a member of the War Cabinet. For a considerable period in the war the Minister of State in the Middle East (Mr. O. Lyttelton followed by Mr. Casey) held office, and Sir Stafford Cripps was a member for a brief period of time in 1942.

A feature of the War Cabinets of both wars was the inclusion of men who were previously not professional politicians, at least in this country. In Mr. Churchill's final War Cabinet only Messrs. Churchill, Eden, Attlee, and Morrison had held membership of the House of Commons before the war. Sir John Anderson (Chancellor of the Exchequer) was a Civil Servant, Mr. Bevin (Minister of Labour) a Trade Union Chief, Mr. Lyttelton (Minister of Production) a City Magnate, and Lord Woolton (Reconstructional) a business man.

In neither war has this feature continued long into times of peace. To quote again from Professor Keith:

"One experiment was made under the War Cabinet system, that of giving Ministries to men not professional politicians. It may fairly be said that its success often was dubious, and in the best cases not distinguished. Government is a business with rules of its own, and is best conducted by men who have made it their life work to familiarize themselves with these rules. The advent of normal government saw the hasty retreat to their normal sphere of the neophytes without leaving any personal contribution of lasting value to the welfare of their people though recognition is due to their eager labour and desire to help their country."

It may be said here, while there is clearly something in what he says, Professor Keith is probably over-stating his case,[1] which was in any event intended to apply only to the First World War. Even in 1915-18 newcomers to high office in this country were in the main, or afterwards became, men of high distinction. In the World War of 1939-45, the newcomers included Mr. Bevin, at present Foreign Secretary, and Mr. Oliver Lyttelton who still remains on the Front Opposition Bench.

---

[1] Nevertheless, Lord Hankey, one of the most experienced living authorities in War Cabinet government, gives it as his opinion that even in the War Cabinet the statesmen must predominate.

CHAPTER X

The Parties

"AFTER ten months of assiduous toil," writes Macaulay in his *History of England*, "the Houses in September, 1641, adjourned for a short vacation. The day on which they met again is one of the most remarkable epochs of our history. From that day dates the corporative existence of the two great parties which have ever since alternatively governed the country. . . ."

"When in October, 1641, the Parliament reassembled after a short recess two hostile parties, essentially the same as those which under different names have ever since contended for the direction of public affairs, appeared confronting each other. During some years they were designated as Cavaliers and Roundheads, they were subsequently called Tories and Whigs. . . . It would not be difficult to compose a lampoon or a panegyric on either of these renowned factions. The truth is, that though both parties have often seriously erred, England could have spared neither.

"If in her institutions, freedom and order, the advantages arising from innovation and the advantages arising from prescription have been combined to an extent elsewhere unknown, we may attribute this happy peculiarity to the strenuous conflicts and alternate victories of two rival confederacies of statesmen, a confederacy zealous for authority and antiquity, and a confederacy zealous for liberty and progress."

Opinions may differ about the date from which the existence of party may be said to date in this country. Redlich in his standard work on the procedure of the House of Commons dates it back to the religious controversies in the reign of Elizabeth.

It is more common to place its origin in the reign of Charles II, and more particularly to the 'seventies of the seventeenth century. It is certain that about that time two organized sections of opinion, the Court and Country party, existed and soon merged into distinct organizations labelling one another by the familiar names of Whig and Tory.

However this may be, Macaulay's account of the philosophy of the party system, and his estimate of the rôles played by the historic British parties and their value to the Commonwealth remains the classic and unequalled exposition of one of the most characteristic and necessary of our political institutions.

In Professor Keith's words:

> "Party is as matters stand the essential mode of working the British Constitution."

Political parties have seldom had a good Press. They have been denounced as conspiracies or caucuses. They have been abused as purely factious confederations always putting their purely sectional interests before that of their country. Froude in his life of Disraeli refers to them as a form of "concealed civil war."

The fact is, however, that Party is one of the characteristic expressions of political liberty and parties have always appeared on the rare occasions in human history when free societies have flourished and human Government has proceeded on the basis of discussion rather than force. A few years after 600 B.C., almost as soon as its first free political institutions were designed, politics in the infant republic of Athens were disputed between two parties, the one Conservative and aristocratic in tendency based on the landed interest, and known from this fact as "the Men of the Plain," the other mercantile and progressive based on the middle-class and the artisan, and known from their interest in overseas trade as the "Men of the Coast." "The two great parties," says J. B. Bury, "were those who were in the main satisfied with the new Constitution, and those who disliked its democratic side and desired to return to aristocratic Government."

Of these two great parties whose struggles in one form or another can be traced right through Athenian history it might have been said, as Macaulay wrote of the two great English parties, "The distinction which then became obvious had always existed, and always must exist. For it has its origin and diversities of temper, of understanding and of interest which are found in all societies. Everywhere there is a class of men who cling with fondness to whatever is ancient, and who, even when convinced of overpowering reasons that innovation would be beneficial, consent to it with many misgivings and forebodings. We find also everywhere another class of men sanguine in hope, bold in speculation, always pressing forward, quick to discern the imperfections of whatever exists, disposed to think lightly of the risks and inconveniences which attend improvements and disposed to consider every change as being an improvement. In the sentiments of both classes there is something to approve. But of both, the best specimens will be found not far from the common frontier. The extreme section of one class consists of bigoted dotards. The extreme section of the other consists of shallow and reckless empirics."

In all countries the normal and healthy party structure divided into two parties, one Conservative and the other Radical, has tended to break down into more numerous groups. In the Athenian policy the Plain and the Coast was joined by a third faction, "the Hill," which promptly proceeded to install a dictator. In the Roman republic the original division between patrician and plebeian, based on class, finally developed into a three-party system, the People's Party, the Conservative and the Mercantile— whose inability to form a stable society was one of the contributory causes of the dictatorship of the Cæsars. In continental democracies the fissiparous tendency of political parties has been carried to far greater lengths, but in each case a prolonged or radical departure from the two-party system has ultimately proved fatal to the liberties of the society concerned. It is among the English-speaking peoples that the party system has reached its greatest development, and it is among these, both here, in the Dominions and in the United States, that on the whole the two-party system has come to be treated most consistently as the norm.

Although political parties in our country can be traced to the period immediately preceding the Civil War, the modern party system dates from the period immediately after the Reform Bill of 1832.

In the General Election of 1831, the Whigs raised funds to finance candidates who advocated reform, thus instituting the fundamental characteristic of the modern political party—the party fund. The Conservatives followed in 1834-35 when a similar central fund was raised, and a ' Conservative Party Organizer appeared under Peel in the person of Lord Granville Somerset.

The second feature of the modern party is the local association. This feature, too, came into being as the result of the passage of measures of Electoral Reform. The first Reform Bill of 1832 added approximately 217,000 voters to the register, and there immediately sprang into being a number of local registration societies acting in the interest of each party, whose chief function was to secure the registration of voters likely to be favourable to the

76

party cause and to oppose the registration of voters of the other faction. The registration of favourable voters continues to be a considerable preoccupation of the modern party agent, even in constituencies where the electorate is too large to enable the result of an election to be greatly swayed by this method.

Two further features of party organization remain to be added, the Central Convention or National Party Conference at the apex of the pyramid and the ward committee or caucus into which the local association is subdivided at its base.

These features were both originally of American origin and owe their introduction in this country to the work of Joseph Chamberlain (at that time a Radical) and his Birmingham manager, Schnadhorst, who introduced the ward system into this country after Disraeli's Reform Bill of 1867 and helped to form the National Liberal Federation in 1877. The Conservatives followed soon after with the National Union of Conservatives and Constitutional Societies which is the direct parent of the present party machine.

The Labour Party presents several distinctive features and has a slightly different history. It originated in several attempts by the trade unions to get separate representation for manual workers within the framework of the existing party system. The first of these attempts was in 1868, and was wholly unsuccessful. The modern Labour Party derives from the Independent Labour Party (formed in 1891) and the Labour Representation Committee formed at the end of 1899, and renamed in 1906 the Labour Party.

Its trade union origin can still be very clearly seen in its constitution. Like the other parties it has local associations and ward committees, but the real control lies not in the hand of individual members acting democratically, but with the corporate members, the trade unions, and the co-operative societies, the latter formally affiliated in 1927.

These practically control the machine. "The vote at Labour Conferences," says the *Economist* (May 13th, 1944), "is determined by the trade unions according to a crudely representative card system. The Labour Politicians as distinct from the trade unions now get the worst of both worlds. Normally the affiliated trade unions are not even affiliated to the local Labour Parties on the basis of individual membership but *en bloc* to the Labour Conference itself. Genuine local Labour membership is minute compared with the votes cast at the Conference." [1]

No account of the organization of the party system would be complete without reference to the way in which the parties are organized inside Parliament. The origin of this organization is lost in time. Presumably the various opposition groups from Stuart days must have had some internal organization, and it is even said that a whip of the King's friends in the early part of the seventeenth century is still acutely extant. The modern system probably dates from the eighteenth century and probably numbers George III among its originators since he formed a separate group in the House of Commons known as "The King's Friends." This group was kept together by something like a modern party organization which apparently sent out written requests or "whips" to attend. Discipline was certainly enforced by means of what would now be called corruption under the Patronage Secretary of the day. It is probably more than a coincidence that although the days of corruption have long since passed, the Chief Government Whip of the present time is still known by the title of "Patronage Secretary."

The modern Parliamentary party is organized through a number of officials known as "Whips" (the metaphor, of course, is from the hunting field). Both the Labour and the Conservative parties have full party meetings with executive committees, but particularly in the Conservative Party the normal organization and discipline is left to the Whips. When the party is in office these are organized under the Patronage Secretary and usually enjoy the minor ministerial offices of "Junior Lords of the Treasury." As Ministers they are entitled to a seat on the Front Bench, but they are not charged with executive functions and seldom speak except to move formal motions or when their personal conduct is called into question. When the party is in opposition the Whips go unpaid, but their existence is formally recognized by the allocation of a separate room for their use equal in size and importance with that enjoyed by the Government Whips.

As organizers of the party machine inside Parliament, the Whips are the "usual channels" (by which name they are invariably referred to in public) whereby one party negotiates with another

---

[1] I am very anxious not to be thought biassed in this estimate. It is the view of practically all acute and independent observers whether or not of Conservative or Socialist views.

about the conduct of public business and the allocation of Government time, and whereby the leaders of a party keep in touch with the opinions of their own rank and file and with other movements of opinion inside the House. The Whips are also responsible for the attendance of members at the time of important divisions. Contrary to what is generally supposed, the Whips do not normally bring direct pressure to bear on a member who wishes to vote against his party, and a threat of action against him is almost never made. The convention is that when a member desires to vote against the party he notifies the Whip, who will try and persuade him by reason not to do so or at least to abstain from voting at all. Where the Whip recognizes that the revolt is general, he will generally be empowered by the party leaders to offer some concession. Direct threats of discipline and promises of advancement are not resorted to, certainly in the Conservative Party, but, in theory at least, a member who habitually votes against the party will lose his membership of the party, and faithful service if combined with ability seldom fails to secure the reward of office.

In the Parliamentary Labour Party the Standing Orders of the Party contain a formal threat of expulsion if a member votes against a party decision. This threat was regularly carried into effect while the Party was in opposition, but may quite probably be allowed to lapse as unpractically severe now that the Party is in power. In like manner, Conservative discipline in opposition may quite easily be strengthened.

Every week the Whips' Office issues a statement of business to party members. This statement is also called "The Party Whip," and withdrawal of the right to receive it constitutes formal excommunication from membership of the party. The "Whip" also contains an exhortation to be present but never a direct request to vote in a particular way.

The "written whip" always employs the following formula in peacetime: "On Tuesday 2 May 1838 the House will meet at 2.45 p.m. to discuss (say) the Budget Resolution Report stage. Your attendance by (say) six o'clock is particularly requested." Where divisions are likely, this is also stated. The degree of importance attached to the member's attendance is indicated by the number of lines with which the words of request are underscored. If no lines are present it may be that his presence is positively unnecessary. One underlining represents business of less than the usual importance. Normal business secures two lines, while three lines indicates that the reason for the member's absence will certainly be made the subject of inquiry.

The form of the whip and underlining it has developed gradually from a date long before the formation of parties.[1] Until quite modern times the whip took the form of a personal letter written to every member in ink and signed by the Chief Whip or Leader of the Party. Such a personal letter at the beginning of the session, signed by Edward Majoribanks (afterwards Lord Tweedmouth), is in my possession. In the Chief Whips Office at 12, Downing Street, is a curious ink-written whip of the time of Disraeli (by which time the modern form was almost fully developed) with no less than four lines underneath the exhortation and the additional phrase "your attendance is *most earnestly* and particularly requested."

In addition to the written statement of business both Government and Opposition Whips "keep doors" throughout the sitting when divisions are expected and try to dissuade their supporters from leaving the House. Sometimes, particularly at the dinner-hour in peacetime, they find this difficult.

Parliament began as a council, established its position as a legislature, proceeded to dominate the executive, and has now let its power largely fall into the grasp of political parties and a Civil Service. The reason is not difficult to see. The Civil Service represents the influence which administration must play in the formation of policy. Party exists as the machine for crystallizing differences of opinion and organizing it into making effective choices. It therefore presents a similar paradox. It is constantly abused, yet it cannot be abolished. It is quite unofficial, yet the official machinery would do none of its work without its assiduous manipulations. Its operation is often contrary to the public interest, yet it is as indispensable to, and as characteristic of, a free society as Parliament itself.

Party is thus the instrument which formulates policy and sup-

---

[1] "Whips underscored by as many as six lines were sent to the King's Friends in the House of Commons as early as 1621. They were issued by the King's Express Command in the Pensioned Parliament, and in the Convention Parliament—even before the beginning of government by Cabinet—parties had their whips. The circulars issued by the administration to its supporters became known as Treasury notes in the reign of George III, seemingly from the fact that they were sent out by the patronage secretary, who by this time was installed in office as chief Government Whip." (Porritt, "The Unreformed House of Commons," i. 509.)

ports leadership in a Government by discussion. Policy viewed as a continuous purpose and as a comprehensive whole given time, is the basis of all intelligent politics. Within the given limitations of time and space a choice must be made between objectives all inherently desirable. Shall the money of the Taxpayer be allowed to fructify in his pockets or go to build the new schools or battleships which the country needs? Or shall it go to give old age pensions of £5 a week? And if all these objectives are impossible of simultaneous realization, on what principle shall we base our inevitable compromise between them? Shall education be a function of parent, state, or county council? Shall it be voluntary or compulsory; how shall we balance our expenditure on this, and our receipts from taxation? All these questions must be built up into an intelligible picture. The picture, when complete, is national policy. When the picture is a complete and intellectually satisfying whole the goal of statesmanship has been reached.

In the painting of this picture Party plays an indispensable part. In this country Party began in Parliament and spread to the constituencies only after the Reform Bill. In the United States it appears to have begun in the constituencies and spread to Congress. But in either event, the purpose is the same. Burke defined the Party as "a body of men united for promoting by their joint endeavours the national interest upon some particular principle in which they are all agreed." He was thinking primarily of the Parliamentary party. A modern political party exercises wide and important functions outside Parliament. First, the disagreements of principle between each party and its opponent serve to crystallize the issues which the electorate must determine at a general election. This function is indispensable. If at a General Election the electorate had to choose between about a thousand and fifteen hundred candidates who had nothing in common with one another but their British nationality, the resulting House of Commons might serve as representative in an exhibition of typical British man and womanhood; but it would rarely represent any significant decision in public affairs. The instrument for formulating the issues, selecting the candidates and choosing the captains and generals in the struggle is Party, and the health or sickness of a democracy is largely measured by the extent to which political parties flourish in vigour but are limited in number. The existence of a multiplicity of parties prevents the electorate from exercising an effective power of choice between practicable alternatives. The absence of parties or, worse still, the reduction in their number to one, effectively prevents the possibility of debate or Government by discussion at all.

Within a Parliament, Party is the instrument for giving effect to policy. No one brain can compass all the multifarious subjects embraced in public affairs. Each man has his own enthusiasm which is apt to obscure for him the balance which must be observed. The man who is interested primarily in the welfare of troops often loses sight of the importance of their winning the battle. The man interested in social welfare often forgets the importance of a prosperous industry. The specialist on foreign affairs loses sight of the importance of the education of the young and the provision of a water supply in the rural areas. Party discipline is the effective check on these legitimate enthusiasms of the individual. It is also his legitimate protection against the importunities of the pressure group. Party loyalty can be, and often is, misused, but it cannot be dispensed with, and, properly understood, is a great help to political integrity. As the 14th Earl of Derby once wrote somewhat caustically to Queen Victoria, "An independent Member of Parliament is a Member of Parliament who cannot be depended upon." This witticism, which was not intended to be taken too literally, for an independent Member must also have an important rôle to play in a fully representative House of Commons, was meant to convey to royal ears the importance of Party in the modern Parliament.

From this extremely sketchy account of the party system in Great Britain certain general conclusions may be drawn.

When we think of the institutions of our country we are apt to conjure up pictures of Church and King, Lords and Commons, Judges and Justices of the Peace, County Councils, Mayors and Corporations, Armies and Fleets, candidates and elections, Cabinets and Civil Servants. But these are only the legal institutions. They are skeleton and bone, not flesh. The truth is that Party is as vital a political institution in this country as Parliament. Without Party, Parliament would wither and decline into a debating club without responsibility, or a *Reichstag* whose business it would be to register approval of the decisions of a dictator or a bureaucracy. Disraeli expressed the same thought in more forceful language: "I say you can have no parliamentary Government if you have no party Government; and therefore when gentlemen denounce party Government they strike at that scheme of Government which in my opinion has made this country great and which I hope will keep it great."

Party within Parliament is the instrument whereby Government retains control of its time and gives coherence and meaning to its policy. In the country at large, Party is the means whereby the public exercises its control over Government. There are always people whose vote at an election is determined by trivial or insignificant considerations. In such minds the great issues of national policy are outweighed by some personal prejudice, interest or predilection. Yet if these were to form the majority it would not be possible to deduce from the result of an election any general inference as to the will of the people on the main issues which it had to determine. Between, say, an anti-vivisectionist, a member of the Farmers' Union and a representative of a particular religious denomination there could be no common policy. A House of Commons elected out of such materials would become a heterogeneous collection of cranky individuals or delegates from various pressure groups free to develop its own programme and to allot office to any combination of its component elements without reference to the opinions of the electorate. A general election yields intelligible results simply because the people are asked a simple and intelligible question. The electors are asked to choose not between the individual merits of about 2,000 candidates or to express opinions about an unco-ordinated series of individual measures. Their choice is between one of two or three possible teams of potential Ministers and between one of two or three coherent legislative programmes. Party is the means whereby this is done. Party is the instrument for the formulation of issues, for the selection of candidates, for the promulgation of policy. In times of emergency coalition between the parties provides the necessary structure upon which national unity can be built in this country. In times of peace it is the means whereby the demand for reform and the criticism of it can be canalized into the channel of orderly discussion. On the whole, the system has served its purposes well.

It may be that the nature of party warfare has often served to obscure its necessary function; that the shifts, ruses and devices of electioneering tend too often to lower the standard which public servants should set themselves; that the need for clear-cut contrasts on election platforms tends too often to denigration and abuse of the opposite side. But all this is on the surface and the necessary check to the evils engendered has long been recognized. This check is the so-called "floating" vote. It has never been true that all the politically-minded have belonged to one party or the other. If it ever became true party politics would degenerate into a feud between Capulets and Montagues. The "floating" vote is as essential to political life in this country as the party system itself and serves to prevent party from degenerating into faction.

"It is also to be noticed," wrote Macaulay in the passage quoted at the beginning of this chapter, "that these two parties have never been the whole nation, nay that they have never taken together made up a majority of the nation. Between them has always been a great mass who has never steadfastly adhered to either, which has sometimes remained inertly neutral and has sometimes oscillated to and fro." The political life of a free country is composed of an infinitely intricate system of counterpoises of which the interaction of the great parties forms an essential but not an all-sufficing part. If the whole were not given form and meaning by the love of country, it would soon degenerate into the chaotic and corrupt alliance of factions and caucuses which characterized the political life of the Third Republic in France.

"A good party man," said Mr. Churchill in the House of Commons when Sir Kingsley Wood died, "is one who puts his party above himself, his country above his party." Such has been the true doctrine from 1641 to the present day.

CHAPTER XI

His Majesty's Opposition

A DISCUSSION of the Cabinet, and of the party system, leads on to a discussion of His Majesty's Opposition, an institution not only almost peculiar to the British Empire but quite unintelligible where there is no Cabinet Government, and no two party system on the Anglo-Saxon model.

In France, where until the war there was Cabinet Government but a multiparty system, there was no opposition as such. Certain party groups were in the Government and certain party groups were outside and trying to get in. Occasionally (not very occasionally) a Government would fall and the mixture in the Cabinet pudding would be slightly varied. But there was neither the inner cohesiveness among supporters of the Government which characterises British Parliamentary majorities, and which makes possible the virtual rule by the Cabinet already noticed, nor was there any single group outside the Government enjoying any special position and prestige by reason of the fact of being an "Official Opposition."

In America, there is likewise no Official Opposition. The President and his Administration depend for their mandate on a popular authority distinct from that of Congress. Often, as at present, they are not of the same political complexion as the majority of one or both of the two Houses. Congress is primarily a legislature, not a "grand inquest of the nation," and a legislature not directed and moulded by the occupants of a Treasury Bench composed wholly of the members of the dominant party.

In the British Constitution His Majesty's Opposition is as definite and as formal a fact as His Majesty's Government, hardly less coherent than the Government, enjoying its own separate life and complete with its own Leader, its own "shadow cabinet," and its own Whips and separate party meetings. The existence of such a group is an integral and indispensable part of our working constitution, and is even so far officially recognized that its titular Leader has been entitled since 1937 to draw an official salary of £2,000 a year.

Here we see in part the influence of the oblong form of Chamber.

From the earliest days it was customary for Privy Councillors and High Officers of State to sit on the two front benches of the House on the right and left of the Speaker.

But ex-Cabinet Ministers are members of the Privy Council as well as the Government, and from the moment that Cabinet Government in its modern form began to appear, that is from soon after 1714, the front bench on the right of the Speaker came to be reserved by unwritten law for Members of the Cabinet and their Ministerial colleagues, and that on the Speaker's left for ex-Ministers and Privy Councillors outside the Government and certain of their friends. The supporters of each group sit on the back benches behind their leaders, so far as numbers and other circumstances permit. We do not know precisely at what date this happened. We can see no trace of it under Queen Anne, although friends presumably then, as now, usually sat together; by 1740 it is fairly clear that something like the present arrangement was fairly widely accepted, but even now the matter is one largely left to the good sense of the House. As late as 1834, William Cobbett somewhat rudely took Sir Robert Peel's seat opposite the despatch box on the front Opposition bench, and in 1944 Sir Richard Acland in the middle of a speech from the back benches below the gangway somewhat melodramatically dashed up the Chamber and took his place at the Opposition despatch box where he went on with his speech. The former outrage was left by the House entirely without redress; the latter, which took place during a speech, was probably out of order, although no very definite ruling was obtained.

Both the name and the fact of "His Majesty's Opposition" date from the early days of the nineteenth century, and the expression has been constantly in use ever since. Strangely, we can fix the actual occasion when the name came into being.

On April 10th, 1826, Mr. Hobhouse (afterwards Lord Broughton) was in opposition to Canning under Tierney, the somewhat ineffective but violent Whig leader. In the course of a somewhat derisive speech Hobhouse used the word. "It was said to be hard on His Majesty's Ministers to raise objections of this character. For his own part he thought it was more hard on His Majesty's Opposition to compel them to take this course."

The happy coinage was welcomed by Canning, and the Whig

leader took it up—but it gave a turn which, somewhat characteristically, deprived it of its finer meaning. "My Right Honourable Friend," he said, "could not have invented a better phrase to designate us than that which he has adopted. For we are certainly to all intents and purposes a branch of His Majesty's Government. Its proceedings for some time past have proved that though the gentlemen opposite are in office, we are in power. The measures are ours, but the emoluments are theirs."

What are the functions of an Opposition? Why is an Opposition necessary? What are its objects, and what methods should it pursue?

To see the necessity of an organized Opposition under the British Cabinet system, it is only necessary to consider what the position would be if the Cabinet and the Government party were the only organized body of opinion in the country or in the House.

In the British Constitution, the Executive possesses a greater power than in any other free country. Without an organized counterpoise to this power the influence of the Cabinet would be such that, without any fresh inroads on our liberty, it would be doubtful to what extent we could legitimately describe ourselves as a free country at all. This, it will be observed, is the main British criticism of the Russian system as seen in Russia itself and certain of the liberated countries under Russian influence. The difference between such systems and the British is not so easy to define in precise or palpable terms. Many of the vital British liberties are preserved, and many delegations visiting the country are pleasantly impressed with visible indications of the popularity and liberalism of the regime. To American eyes the picture would be hopelessly shocking. British critics will content themselves with a single observation. In our sense such countries cannot be fully free until they have an organized Opposition. It is not a long step from the absence of an organized Opposition to a complete dictatorship.

It must be remembered that Party is not merely an institution of democracy. In modern dictatorships of Right and Left the expression "the party" assumes a new and sinister significance. In some ways the party in this sense does not differ from its opposite number in a democracy. It promulgates policy, formulates issues, conducts public discussion, operates to select and publicize leaders and leadership, combines to overthrow opposition and to resist separatist tendencies. It is the same institution but has been made to serve purposes fundamentally different. Partly this difference lies in the absence of any rival. Under authoritarian rule only one party can be permitted to exist. "The Party" is to the citizen what the priesthood is to a corrupt church, the one means of promotion, the single authorized vehicle of grace, the sole recognized dispenser of truth, tolerating neither heresy nor schism, claiming as its privilege alike the prerogative of Cæsar and the infallibility of the Godhead.

In a democracy a party exists to serve its members, and through them, the nation. A totalitarian party exists to exact service and to subordinate the nation to the will of its leaders. It is not merely a persecuting Church. It also claims to be a universal religion, and a King by Divine Right.

British Policy is the product not, as is generally supposed, simply of majority rule, but of government by discussion, of the interplay between the Opposition's reasoning and objection, and the Government majority in the lobbies. The power of the organized minority[1] should by no means be ignored for good or ill. Under Parliamentary institutions, majority or no majority, a Government has not absolute power, and its policy is always the product of the impact of the principles of an Opposition on its own principles. If a Government with pacifist or socialist principles be in power, its policy will still be the product of discussion in Parliament with the members of the party opposite. Successive Governments enjoying enormous majorities and nominally committed to private enterprise have produced programmes plainly influenced by comparatively small minorities with a more socialistic outlook. One of the first acts of a Labour Government was to issue an announcement of the industries which were *not* going to be socialized.

This leads us to the consideration of a very important aspect of the British party system—in part a consequence of its successful working, but much more definitely a condition of its successful working. In the words of Professor Keith,[2] "It is an essential feature of the British Party system that the parties should be agreed on fundamentals, in special (*sic*) on the principle of majority rule under a democracy, and the reason of the degree of

---

[1] I do not mean by this the individual complaints of back-benchers. The hey-day of the private Member fighting a lone hand has certainly passed.
[2] "The British Cabinet System," p. 320.

success attained in its operation lies simply in this consideration. In foreign countries where the British model has been copied it has worked only where a like guiding doctrine is accepted, as in Holland, Belgium and the Scandinavian states. Where the doctrine has received only lip service the result is that the system does not work."

It is this factor which Froude failed to take into account when he described "party Government" as "a concealed form of civil war." It is not a form of civil war; it is a substitute for it, and it is this which justifies its rancour and at the same time explains the self-imposed limitations which it respects. If it were not rancorous, deep divisions of opinion would be unrepresented. If it did not stop short of actual violence, if it did not shrink from organized and meaningless obstruction, if it did not positively co-operate and assist the Government in times of national danger or in certain cases of internal crisis, it would fail to be a substitute for mutual destruction which it is the peculiar purpose and glory of the British Constitution to prevent.

Here again the pageant serves to symbolize the reality. The Opposition leaders, no less than Cabinet Ministers, are members of His Majesty's most honourable Privy Council. Opposition Members of Parliament, no less than supporters of the Government subscribe to the Oath of Allegiance. It is His Majesty's Opposition, not a rump, a faction, or a caucus. Bitter invective, hard-hitting criticism, sharp irony, are its legitimate weapons. But in Britain opposition is still a function of the public service, and the best brains of both parties all sincerely believe, and act in the belief that parties exist to serve a country, and not a party to serve parties.

This theory of "responsible Opposition" marks as superficial and unduly cynical Lord Randolph Churchill's aphorism that the function of the Opposition is to oppose. Its real function is more subtle. It is to act as the responsible outlet for criticism, as the incorruptible searcher after scandals which need exposure, the organized expression of legitimate grievances, and last but not least, to act as a partly-formed, trained, responsible team prepared to take office as a Government when the existing administration loses the confidence of the people. British Government is thus based on the team spirit, and this is one of the many reasons why, when a Government falls, the British people prefer to see a clean sweep and a new team in, rather than a rearrangement of the old figures with a few omissions and additions on the Continental model.

This train of thought is not mere philosophizing. It is a fair statement of the conduct of Oppositions at their best throughout their Parliamentary history of nearly a century and a half.

"As matters stand," says Professor Keith,[1] "as both great parties, as well as the Liberals, still cling to democracy, there are definite limits which they must respect. The Opposition seeks power to effect the changes it desires, but it does not seek power by means which deny democracy. There are standards of fair dealing which are normally respected, and which, if any party should violate, it endeavours to prove still in reality intact. It follows, therefore, that in many matters there must be co-operation above all in arranging the business of the House. It is not the right of the Government to stifle criticism; it must, therefore, put down for discussion such financial items as the Opposition wish to discuss. It must find time for the discussion of a vote of censure. On the other hand, it expects reasonable aid from the Opposition in dealing with normal non-contentious business and in arranging the use of Parliamentary time. It is entitled to be free from meaningless obstruction intended simply to waste the session. . . . The measure of co-operation must vary with the occasion. It is closest in war or time of threat of war. . . . Co-operation is also sought when issues approach such a crisis that inaction would be dangerous to the public welfare." It would seem to be established usage now that in moments of supreme national crisis the members of both parties unite in a national coalition to save their country; it is none the less established usage, it would appear, that when the crisis is over the parties should separate into the normal conflicting teams composed of a party Cabinet and His Majesty's Opposition.

Dr. Jennings[2] analyses the electoral basis for the peculiar relations between Opposition and Government—an analysis which has only been confirmed by the General Election of 1945, which took place after the publication of his book.

Now that Eire is excluded from the Imperial Parliament, there are in this country no clearly-cut classes or communities (except perhaps in mining areas) which are irreconcilable to the aims of either one party or the other. There is no absolute division as

[1] *Op. cit.*, p. 321.
[2] "Parliament," p. 152 ff.

there is in Ulster between Protestant and Catholic—or between Moslem and Hindu in India, or Jew and Arab in Palestine. There is, as Macaulay observed, an enormous "floating vote." "An analysis of election returns," says Dr. Jennings, "shows that at every election since 1884 (the Election of 1918 excepted) the electorate has been divided into two almost equal camps for and against the Government. The chief Opposition party has usually secured a somewhat lower vote than the Government, but the difference is never very great. . . . In 1935, less than 500,000 votes properly distributed would have given the Labour Party a majority."

We may add that in 1945 a transfer of only about a million votes, properly distributed, led to a complete reversal of the position between the two parties. A Parliament which was composed of 400 Conservatives and 200 Labour members was succeeded by a Parliament composed of 200 Conservatives and 400 Labour members.

The result is that both parties are really concerned with two, to some extent, inconsistent objectives. The first is to prevent a split in their own ranks, the second to secure the floating vote. The first drives them towards extremes, since the Conservative Party is more likely to hive off to the Right (as in 1846) and the Labour Party to the Left (as in 1931). The second, happily, drives them towards moderation. "During elections," observes Dr. Jennings, "the right becomes strangely progressive, and the left strangely Conservative. The purpose of parliamentary opposition is, therefore, to appeal to the floating vote. The Opposition does not expect to be able to turn out the Government by its vote. It hopes to persuade the floating vote to do so at the next election. . . . The Opposition is compelled by the logic of the Parliamentary system to adopt a responsible attitude. It is not only His Majesty's Opposition but also His Majesty's alternative Government. It presents itself to the electorate in that capacity. It asks for a mandate to govern. It must show its capacity to govern in the parliamentary arena. . . . All oppositions are, to their opponents, factions and irresponsible. But the word goes round whether they are good or bad."

CHAPTER XII

The Civil Service

SITTING in the House of Commons, weary Members often consult the clock above the Speaker's Chair.

This clock is set in the gallery which supports the Press and members of the Public. Under the gallery, and on the Floor of the House itself are two boxes rather like the boxes in a theatre, but flat. These are technically outside the House and contain only spectators of the debate.

The box on the Opposition side contains members of the public who are lucky enough to secure a seat. If ever you know of a schoolboy who wants to see the House of Commons for the first time, get him a seat under the gallery. A gallery seat gives the impression of being a spectator at a theatre, or perhaps at a bull-fight or a football match. But under the gallery the queer irresistible magic atmosphere of the House of Commons swirls up and grips you by the throat like a November fog. You are in it, and almost of it. Some of the participants are so close to you that you could poke them with your walking-stick (if you had been allowed to retain it). You hear their whispered comments to one another, their not-so-whispered conversation during a dull speech. Their ejaculations and interruptions bombinate on the ear like the sounds of battle (which is just what they are).

But no schoolboy is allowed to penetrate the other similar gallery on the Government side (one once was, and he is writing this, but he must have been almost the only one). This gallery is occupied to capacity by a group of earnest, attentive, brilliant, hard-working, ill-dressed little men and women whose faces never betray the smallest sympathy or amusement at what is going on, but whose hearts at times must beat with the same sort of emotion as the trainer of a racehorse when he sees his animal fall down on the course.

For this is the gallery of the Civil Servants. From time to time an anxious Minister will rise from his place to seek enlightenment on an awkward point raised by a Member of the Opposition or perhaps send his "PPS" to get a few facts on a particular subject. The Civil Servants supply the necessary brief to enable the

Government (of whatever political persuasion) to defeat its opponents. It is one of the many weapons in the hand of the Executive which enables Britain, though a democracy, to be governed. The three or four men sitting in the gallery are the only portion visible to Parliament of one of the most flexible and brilliantly conceived organizations of modern times, or of any times: the British Civil Service—an expression which I here use for convenience to describe both this and the separate but cognate Foreign Service.

Unlike most of our institutions, the Civil Service is something of very modern growth. Public officials there have been, of course, from the very earliest times. But in the main these received their offices by favour of the great, and performed their functions unassisted by a highly complex and expert staff. They were at once Ministers and Civil Servants in one, and their tenure of office was as precarious as is of necessity any political appointment. The case of Pepys, a true Civil Servant, was unusual.

Mr. W. J. Brown, in his booklet on the subject, observes that less than one hundred and fifty years ago the number of public officers employed was 15,882, covering fifty-three departments. According to the latest Treasury returns the number of Civil Servants as at October 1st, 1945, was 701,434, not including Foreign Service, Colonial Service and India Office.

These numbers are slightly misleading. Of the 15,882, a goodly number must have been placemen, serving little or no useful purpose. Of the 701,434, a great number represent officials of war-time departments which are likely to disappear. Moreover, in each case a very large number of both totals will represent the particular type we mean when we speak of Civil Servants.

None the less, the Civil Service has grown in a century from a numerically insignificant band of officials to an industry strictly comparable in numbers, though rather smaller, to coal mining or textiles. [1]

The development of the Civil Service has not been a matter of mere numbers. The modern Civil Service may be said to date from the series of reforms which, stretching over something more than fifty years, abolished sinecures, forbade the employment of deputies, unified the conditions of service, and instituted recruitment by examination in place of patronage, and finally produced

---

[1] But if the local government and other public services are taken into account the functionaries are the largest single class in the community.

93

the present instrument—non-political, permanent in the main, its members remunerated by seniority, ill-paid but relatively well-pensioned, selfless, honourable, loyal, unmentioned and usually underrated, efficient, but somewhat lacking in initiative, preferring irony to rhetoric, self-controlled, a trifle colourless, hard-working, a little unambitious, subtle, but unduly impressed with administrative difficulty, painstaking, sure-footed, methodical, phlegmatic—they are typically British in everything except their unnatural patience with politicians, who are at once their natural enemies and their masters.

The Civil Service is as much a necessity to Parliamentary democracy as the ballot box. The essence of Parliamentary government, especially where the franchise is democratic, is the establishment of completely unqualified persons in positions of considerable power. In the nature of things, before he has had time to learn all the intricacies of his office a Minister is swept off to some new department. Although changes of Government are not as frequent in Great Britain as in some Continental democracies, Government reshuffles on a greater or smaller scale occur in peace-time every few months.

In such circumstances Parliamentary Government could not achieve even the most elementary efficiency (and administratively speaking we are probably the most efficient country in the world) were it not for the existence of highly-skilled permanent staff whose function it is to translate into practice the political demands of their ephemeral masters.

The Civil Service has thus become a power in the democratic state, although it remains, in the nature of things, a power behind the scenes. The Civil Service represents the influence which administration must necessarily possess in the formation of policy in a modern state. Bismarck defined politics as the art of the possible. The Civil Servant exists to translate the impossible demands of politician and populace into the actuality of effective government. He is thus alike the politicians' natural enemy and indispensable ally—natural enemy because it is he who provides the unruffled evasions and the practical objections which form the Minister's Siegfried line of defence against importunate back-benchers—indispensable ally because without his patient, loyal and unselfseeking co-operation none of the aspirations or ideals of the politician would be worth the breath in which they are expressed.

The Civil Service

The Home Civil Service is hierarchical in structure. The Civil Servant is often compared to one of the social insects—the termite, the ant, or the bee. And it is certainly true that the inner structure of the Civil Service constantly reminds one of the highly differentiated classes in some highly developed species of termitary. There are hewers of wood and drawers of water in the subclerical grades, hundreds of thousands of clericals, executives (mildly injected with the Royal jelly), and administrative officials, about twelve hundred in all, alone able to hold the highest appointments and play an important part in the formulation of policy.

As the function of the Civil Service is to implement the policy of the Government, it is essential that it should be, and remain, non-political. Membership of a political party is not forbidden to its members—but the higher the official, the more objectional party ties become, and in the lower grades the law as it stands at present is that in their organized capacity as trade unionists Civil Servants may not affiliate to a political party or the Trade Union Conference.[1]

In this respect our own Civil Service differs, and differs for the better, from the American. American public life has long been marred by what has come to be known as the "Spoils" system. We are accustomed to a change of Government meaning a change in all the political offices associated with the High Departments of State. But we do not expect to see a new postman or a new dustman calling at the door when a Labour Government is elected to power. This is scarcely a caricature of what used to happen until comparatively recently under the Spoils system. For some years now, however, the American system of administration has been slowly moving over towards a Civil Service like ours—unpolitical, like ours permanent, and like ours appointed by ability.

None the less, even now the United States have not yet made it the rule to appoint "career diplomats" normally as ambassadors.

Do the Civil Service rule the Government or does the Government rule the Civil Service? Many times in recent years cynics have observed: "It doesn't matter whom you've got in power—Liberals, Conservatives, or Labour. It all amounts to the same thing. These little jacks in office come and go, but the real work of Government is done by the Civil Service."

This cynicism contains just enough truth to make it thoroughly

---

[1] Since I wrote this the repeal of the Trade Disputes Act of 1927 has removed this legal disability.

misleading. A Government which had not at its command a thoroughly efficient Civil Service could not perform the functions of Government at all. This, and not constitutional inefficiency, is one of the reasons why at the beginning of a war, when the whole instrument of Government is lacking for certain vital wartime purposes, nearly all Governments have failed.

Moreover, it is the business of a permanent staff to point out the difficulties and objections from an administrative point of view to a course of policy proposed by a Minister. If they did not do this they would simply not be doing their job. But to represent the Civil Service either negatively as seeking to wreck policies of which they disapprove, or positively as initiating great new policies they support despite objections from their Minister—is at best to misrepresent reality and at worst to traduce gravely a devoted body of men.

The whole genius of the civil servant is that he remains a servant—the loyal subordinate of the Minister, the unselfish servant of the Crown. Again to quote Mr. W. J. Brown: "There is a real sense in which the Civil Service is a vocation, a kind of priesthood." It would be a bad civil servant who tried to manage his Minister, and only a very bad Minister who tries to avoid responsibility by leaving his department a policy dictated only by the Civil Service. Each has a different function, and only when each performs his function well can the whole machine of Government function as it should.

Partly because it cannot as such answer for itself, and partly because it must always, from its very nature, prepare a defence for Ministers to deliver, of every administrative mistake, or for the retention of almost every anomalous *status quo*, the Civil Service has a bad Press. Its great virtues, its loyalty, its incorruptibility, and its almost incomparable efficiency are largely forgotten, and in its place is drawn a caricature of a bone-headed, rigid, pedantic, inhuman, formalistic bureaucracy which is anything but commonsense, efficient, and flexible.

To some extent the caricature has an element of truth. We all have the defects of our qualities, and the caricatures of almost all professions have enough truth to make them recognizable. Lawyers *are* fond of arguing both ways. Soldiers *do* make absurdly unreflective remarks beginning: "Good God! Sir!" or worse. Parsons *are* often affected, and "parsonical." Politicians *do* try to be all things to all men. Business men *are* sometimes flint-faced and avaricious. Workers are frequently unreasonable and rapacious.

But it is absurd to mistake the qualities which go with the defects. The civil servant's job is to see that administrative anomalies are ironed out. He is apt, therefore, to remind us when we least wish to be reminded that hard cases make bad law. If he is a Treasury official, it is his business to see that public money is not squandered, and that the demands of a spending department manned by a go-getting and ambitious politician do not exceed out of all proportion what other departments, whose needs may be equally insistent if less ably advocated, are getting. It is his business to leave an adequate record in the form of a minute of every significant action, and to see that all the appropriate sections are consulted or at least informed.

When all is said and done, if we had no Civil Service we should have no democracy, and the British Civil Service is incomparably the most honest, efficient and public spirited a service that a great country has ever enjoyed.

CHAPTER XIII

The Press, Wireless, and the Strangers' Gallery

WHEN Jeremy Bentham wrote his "Essay on Political Tactics," a treatise on the theory of Parliamentary procedure, the first principle he enunciated was that of publicity.

"Before entering into the detail of the operations of the assembly let us place at the head of the regulations the fittest law for securing the public confidence and causing it constantly to advance towards the end of its institution. This law is that of *publicity*."

The reasons for the fullest publication of debates are often ignored: that they should be so ignored is always a sign of some grave evil in the body politic, and the only exception, the secret sessions held during a war, is the symptom of perhaps the greatest evil of all.

"The public," says Bentham, "compose a tribunal which is more powerful than all the other tribunals together. . . . The enemies of publicity may be collected into three classes: the malefactor, who seeks to escape the notice of the judge; the tyrant, who seeks to stifle public opinion, while he fears to hear its voice; the timid or indolent man, who complains of the general incapacity in order to screen his own."

Among the purposes of publicity in the practice of a free Parliament, Bentham gives four of major importance:—

To constrain the members of the assembly to perform their duty.

To secure the confidence of the people.

To enable the governors to know the wishes of the governed.

To educate the electorate.

"Suspicion," he cries, "always attached to mystery."

"In an open and free policy, what confidence and security, I do not say for the people but for the governors themselves. Let it be impossible that anything should be done which is unknown to the nation. Prove to it that you neither intend to deceive nor to surprise—you take away all the weapons of discontent. The public will repay with usury the confidence you repose in it."

To these advantages a modern writer might properly add a fourth—good public relations. In the heat and bitterness of the party struggle, when each side abuses its opponents, there is a danger that each will be believed in that part of their case which consists in calumnies against their rivals—with the inevitable result that the institutions of Parliamentary democracy themselves may be brought into disrepute, and the name of Parliament abused.

To counter this in the long run, the only weapon is publicity. Let the public see and hear what actually goes on in Parliament. Let them learn to distinguish for themselves the value and the power of free discussion in an assembly where each is free to speak his mind, but subject to the requirements of a rigid discipline in deportment. There is no better antidote to the general attack on the motives and personalities of members of a political party than to let them speak for themselves in an assembly where they are open to the freest criticism. British public life has nothing to fear from such an exposure.

It is paradoxical that although the British Parliament is the freest and most publicized assembly in the world—not excluding the Congress of the United States—in theory the principle of publicity has never been conceded by either House of Parliament.

Hooker, writing in Elizabeth's day, remarks in effect that every session of the House of Commons was in effect a secret session.

"Also every person of the Parliament ought to keep secret and not to disclose the secrets and things done and spoken in the Parliament House to any manner of person, unless he be one of the same house, upon pain to be sequestered out of the house, or otherwise be punished as by the order of the house shall be appointed."

Nevertheless the journals of the House were regularly kept from the earliest times, as the Minutes of any other Society, and we have a fairly complete set from 1547 onwards. These, of course, were for record and not for inspection or perusal by the public.

The earliest of these sometimes contained a fairly full note of the speeches; but this was considered unsafe as relations with the Crown grew more strained. This is particularly so after the famous episode when King James I read the journal of the House, and was so angry at what it contained that he ripped out the page with his own royal hand—an outrage faithfully reported by an industrious clerk on the very next page of the book.

In 1628, therefore, the House resolved that no notes of speeches should be taken, and on April 15th, 1640, on the eve of Civil War, it was found necessary to forbid Rushworth the assistant clerk to take any notes without express directions, apart from the orders and reports made. From this time onward the journal of the House becomes the dry, staccato and formal record of business done which nobody reads to-day.[1]

From 1641, however, Parliament began to take steps to see that at least this bare record of its proceedings should be known and published. And from March 24th, 1680-1681 the House began a procedure which it continues to the present day of making a general order at the beginning of each sessions for the printing and publication of all its votes and proceedings.

The actual speeches of Members continued to be technically secret until a much later period. In Queen Elizabeth's day Members kept private diaries which have since found their way into print, and the general character of proceedings was always fairly well known in the capital. After the Restoration, Members such as Marvell "made a profession of furnishing notes of the debates, obviously with the tacit approval of the House."[2]

It was characteristic of the eighteenth century that the practice of the House was somewhat less liberal than that which immediately preceded it ; the journalism of the Coffee-house prints had just begun, and the House of those days was fairly generally agreed to treat their contributors as their natural enemies.

In 1738, for instance, a resolution of the House of Commons decided that it was—

"A high indignity to, and a notorious breach of privilege of this House for any newswriter in letters or other papers (as minutes or under any other denomination) to insert in the said letters or papers or to give therein any account of the debates or other proceedings of this House or any Committee thereof as well during the recess as the sitting of Parliament; and that this House will proceed with the utmost severity against such offenders. . . ."

This resolution was repeated in 1753 and 1762, and in the 'seventies of the same century the principle of publicity had its martyrs in the distinguished persons of the Lord Mayor and two aldermen of the City of London who were actually committed to

---

[1] Cf. Redlich, ii., p. 36.
[2] *Ibid.*

prison for contempt of the House during the bitterness engendered by the Wilkes dispute.

In practice, however, Parliament was quite unable to stem the tide. Among the earliest lobby correspondents was Dr. Johnson himself, who contributed the Parliamentary news for the *Gentleman's Magazine*. The only trouble with all these reports is that we do not know how much was fact and how much intelligent guessing. Some, no doubt, was deliberate fiction. Dr. Johnson, it will be remembered, was careful to see that in his reports the Whig dogs did not get the best of it, and no doubt his less eminent contemporaries in the lobby were no more scrupulous.

From 1770 onwards the House of Commons ceased to persecute actively the correspondents of the Press, and Parliamentary reports from now on begin to diverge into three main streams of activity—the specialized report of Parliamentary proceedings, which ultimately developed into the modern official report, or *Hansard* as it may now again be called officially, the general report found in the columns of the better-class newspapers, and the sketches of Parliament and Parliamentary gossip emanating from the regular lobby correspondents and varying from the most biassed and distorted accounts to the best informed political gossip of the day.

There has been a reporters' gallery in the House of Lords since 1831, and in 1835 a gallery in the House of Commons was set aside for this purpose. The present gallery in the House of Lords is very inadequate for the requirements. Even the old House of Commons gallery accommodated less than sixty persons, and already by 1908 Redlich was writing: "After providing for the leading London dailies and a few important provincial papers, there are only a very few seats left for the great news agencies." The new House, it is to be hoped, will be more commodious.

One good legacy from the bad old days of want of publicity remains. The distribution of places in the limited reporters' gallery is controlled, and places are still in the hands of the Serjeant at Arms under the general tutelage of the Speaker. This gives the members of the lobby a strong corporate sense. They are a highly responsible, highly trusted, and, it must be added, a highly paid body of men. Their job is not only to reprint what goes on in public, but to learn what goes on behind the scenes. They are admitted to the Members' lobby and very little escapes their attention. In my experience the best way to keep a secret in

Parliament is to go straight to the reporters and tell them every-thing under the seal of confidence; confession is good for the soul, and if you are in time your confidence will be respected. Every year a few fortunate Members, and a few distinguished Ministers are lunched by the lobby correspondents at a well-known hotel. The things that are said at that lunch in the speeches and across the table would shake dynasties and rock the country. But not a word ever leaks out into the Press.

The history of the Official Reports is also interesting. Like most else in the country it was long carried on as a private business. The present Official Report is the lineal descendant of reports published as a sequel to his history by William Cobbett, and was originally printed for him by a Mr. T. C. Hansard.

In 1803 [1] *Hansard* took the responsibility of compiling the series and from 1803 to 1855 he and his firm continued to produce the reports merely as a private venture. In 1855 came the first official recognition in the shape of an order for 100 copies daily from the Treasury, and in 1877 in return for a somewhat fuller account a direct subsidy of £300 afterwards increased from time to time, was paid. In 1891 the name *Hansard* was dropped (it has since been revived as a conscious archaism), and in 1908 the Official Report appeared at last as an undertaking entirely owned and controlled by the nation and directly employed by the House of Commons.

The publication of these reports is a considerable feat of organization. A full verbatim report of everything that goes on is taken in relays by a trained staff of reporters, and dictated on to a typewriter during the entire progress of the debate, as each reporter leaves the table. A printed version is in the hands of the public in paper covers by ten o'clock the following morning in peace-time,[2] and a corrected and more accurate print is bound up in a permanent record at regular intervals.

Hansard is not free, especially in wartime, from verbal errors, some of them serious. A certain amount of improvement of style is done by the reporters themselves in the course of their dictation and to some remarks they remain conveniently and discreetly deaf. But *Hansard* is essential to the student or Member of Parliament. Even the fullest of Press reports fails to convey the

---

[1] Cf. Redlich, ii., 31.

[2] At present it still does not cover the whole of the day's proceedings if the House sits after 9.15 p.m.

full flavour and balance of the verbatim report. Members, if they are wise, go up to the reporters' gallery after making an important speech and correct the typescript notes of the reporter before the daily version is printed. They must, however, limit themselves to an improvement of the style and correction of errors in the transcript. The House is extremely jealous of any attempt to alter in the smallest degree the actual sense of what was said.

A new principle in the scheme of publicity is the B.B.C., and, at least in the opinion of the writer, the medium of broadcasting has already ousted the Press and the Official Report as the main source from which the public draw their information concerning the proceedings in Parliament.

Characteristically enough, and entirely in keeping with its tradition in this matter, the House has approached the new medium with great caution. Until 1945 the B.B.C. was denied the advantage of an official lobby correspondent, and the accounts of Parliament broadcast in the official News bulletin are still based on the ticker tape. This is unsatisfactory as such a report, although fairly full, is still limited and unbalanced and the scissors and paste version which is ultimately broadcast sometimes seriously interrupts the flow and sense of the discussion.

In addition to the news bulletins, the B.B.C. have for some time organized a feature called the "Week in Westminster," broadcast during the sittings of the House by selected Members of Parliament (usually, but not always, Members of the House of Commons) and some lobby correspondents. The difficulty of this feature is that it necessarily gives only the speaker's own subjective picture, and with the re-introduction of party politics in 1945 some of the broadcasts give too tendentious a tinge to what is said. This is a perversion, because although the B.B.C. is always scrupulously careful to select their speakers from all parties and even to balance their selection as between different sections of the same party, a series of reports which are all biassed from different points of view does not add up to a series of unbiassed reports. The real purpose of this feature should be the justification and explanation of Parliament as an institution, and it should not be treated as a proper vehicle of party propaganda.

In addition to these two features, and to a generous use of M.P.'s in their general broadcasting policy, the B.B.C. also runs a late nightly feature conducted by their Parliamentary representative called "In Parliament To-day," the object of which is to put the spotlight on the temporary activities. This is a most valuable feature and does much good in popularizing Parliament.

Should the debates in Parliament be broadcast? For some years now the debates in the New Zealand House of Commons have been broadcast, but in Britain all attempts to introduce broadcasting have been met by a general conservatism—which in matters affecting House of Commons procedure is not less characteristic of Left than Right wing parties.

The question is not without its difficulties. To begin with, it would be manifestly wrong to broadcast parts of a debate, and not the whole of it, for this must give an unbalanced picture and an unfair advantage to those whose necessarily controversial speeches were broadcast. The whole debate must be broadcast if at all, and this means in practice that a special wavelength would have to be set aside for the purpose, since the ordinary listening public quite obviously do not wish Dr. Joad and ITMA to be permanently excluded from the air to make way for a long desert of political controversy.

Moreover, Members of the House of Commons would claim, as their predecessors claimed when Press reporting was a controversial subject, and perhaps with more reason, that the presence of the microphone would ruin the House as a debating assembly. Even now Members of experience recognize the man who is speaking not to the House but to the reporter of his local paper up in the gallery as a signal to go out for a cup of tea at once, and they might reasonably fear that such speeches—to the unseen millions who listen for five and ten minutes, and not to the debate—would ruin the character of the House as a debating chamber.

New Zealanders with whom I have spoken on this important topic are divided. Some speak enthusiastically of the experiment, others say that it has spoiled the character of the debate, and that the practice leads to undesirable competition to catch the Speaker's eye at the peak broadcasting hour.

My own opinion, not that it matters, is that the "ayes" have it; this means, if I am right, that it will eventually come to pass—in about a hundred and fifty years' time. Whatever their politics, Parliament men are apt to be a little conservative in anything affecting their personal habits.

The subject of publicity naturally raises the question of the visitors' gallery. In theory it followed from the fact that proceedings were technically secret, that no stranger could be allowed in the House of Commons, and in Elizabethan and Stuart days the delicacy of the relations between the House and the Crown led to the rule being severely observed. Moreover, in Elizabeth's day, intruders were suspected of being Catholic spies,[1] and, in addition to imprisonment for contempt, they were usually called upon to take the Oath of Supremacy. Resolutions insisting on compliance were passed in 1688 and 1689. The practice subsequently became a sessional order.

There was, however, a gallery in the old House of Commons (as we see from many prints) and these and the emphasis laid on the gallery in some of the resolutions, shows that the rule was disobeyed fairly frequently, and that the gallery was the normal place where such infringements took place. Even ladies are depicted and described as listening to debates from this place, but they were expressly excluded between 1778 and 1834, and could from that time onwards only listen through the ventilator in the roof chamber above the House in the Old St. Stephen's Chapel. By a curious piece of archaism Barry constructed a ladies' gallery on the same principle as the ventilator high up in the roof and behind a grille in the pre-1941 Chamber, but ladies soon afterwards were allowed into the public galleries, and so were better off than the men.

Barry's House of Commons contained inadequate accommodation for strangers, but a fairly commodious gallery for Members, for Peers, and for the Speaker's friends. In the converted House of Lords strangers' tickets are very difficult to obtain. They are allotted by ballot a week in advance, and as, after the various official galleries have been removed, only about thirty-three seats remain, the chances of success in the ballot for two places (the number normally allotted) are negligible for any one day. Later in the debate, when interest has subsided, tickets can usually be obtained by a Member for his friends and constituents during the duller parts of the debate.

The proposals for the new House will contain somewhat better accommodation for strangers than has ever been enjoyed before.

The right to exclude strangers from the gallery at will was last used in the 'seventies of the last century. On April 27th, 1875, it was attempted by an Irish obstructionist when Disraeli moved and carried the suspension of the Standing Order. From then on

---

[1] Cf. Redlich, ii. 34-5.

the practice when a Member "spies strangers" has been to interrupt the business of the House while a division is held deciding whether strangers should remain.

In time of war this ancient procedure of spying strangers was the method adopted to achieve the holding of the necessary secret sessions—a characteristic archaism of which the House of Commons was conscious and proud.

The Prime Minister, desiring to communicate something to the House which could not be said in public, used the time-honoured formula: "Mr. Speaker, I beg to draw your attention to the fact that strangers are present."

The Speaker thereupon said "The question is that the strangers do withdraw," and proceeded to put the question.

When the "strangers" which included all the occupants of the gallery, even the civil servants and official reporters (but not peers) had withdrawn, the Prime Minister moved:

"That the rest of the proceedings this day be held in secret session," and it became the duty of Members of Parliament as in Hooker's day, "to keep secret and not to disclose the secrets and things done and spoken in the Parliament House." This obligation was with one or two possible and unintentional exceptions honourably observed, although I may say that in most of the Secret Sessions which I attended[1] little enough was usually disclosed except hours of sitting and the movements of important personages. There were, however, occasions when speeches were made which could not have been made in public. One secret session was held on tanks about the time of the invasion of Europe; one (which I did not attend owing to military service abroad) had to do amongst other things with the sinkings in Alexandria harbour, and in one, certain statements were made about the American attitude in the event of our refusing to close the Burma Road in 1940. All the proceedings in the secret sessions, apart from the absence of official reporters and of the civil servants to brief the Ministers from their seats under the gallery, were held according to the ordinary procedure of the House of Commons.

---

[1] Members are now by order of the House at liberty to disclose what happened.

CHAPTER XIV

What Happens at Elections

IN the summer of 1938 I was spending a holiday with a friend in Scotland when I read in my newspaper that Captain Bourne, M.P., the talented and popular Member for Oxford City, had died suddenly while on a walk with his family.

My friend suggested that I should apply to be selected as Conservative candidate in the by-election that was to be held. I was doubtful at first. It seemed to me that Oxford City would be likely to choose a far better-known and more mature standard bearer than myself. However, I loved Oxford, and hoped I might be found worthy to serve.

I had long contemplated seeking election to the House of Commons, and I knew exactly what had to be done. I obtained the address of the chairman of the local association. I wired my willingness to let my name go forward, and wrote a letter giving my name, age, experience and qualifications. The Conservative Central Office had already approved my name as a suitable candidate, and so, if selected, I should have been free to stand.

Immediately they are aware of an impending or actual vacancy it is the business of the local party association to appoint a Selection Committee whose business it is to select one or two names for submission to the executive as a prospective candidate. In some cases they receive up to sixty applications from various sources.

Their first task is to weed these out to arrive at a "short list" for interview. This is usually not difficult. The short list will probably not exceed half a dozen at the most. My own application was received after the short list was prepared, and I was selected for interview when the possible rivals had already been narrowed down to one. This had happened to me once before, so I knew the form fairly well.

The interview consists in the candidate appearing before the Committee. He may be asked for a brief statement of his views or he may be subjected to question and answer for a long period of time. In my own case on each occasion my rival and I were invited to attend the meeting at the same hour, and we were left to spend what seemed a considerable time in the waiting-room to entertain each other with somewhat stilted conversation.

If selected, the aspirant has two more fences to jump. The Selection Committee may have selected him as their sole recommendation to the Executive, or he may have one or more rivals. He will be expected in either event to make a speech and answer more questions from them. This is perhaps the most alarming stage of the proceedings. If he gets past the Executive Committee, which may consist of thirty or forty people, things will be made easy for him at the General Meeting which finally adopts him.

Up to this point none of the legal machinery has been set in motion. The other parties will be engaged in a similar attempt to select their own candidates, and independent groups may be getting together to put forward a candidate of their own. In my own case I found a Liberal and Labour candidate already in the field against me, but both horses were scratched at the last minute, and the two party Executive Committees joined together to support a candidate nominally independent but in reality representing a coalition of three or four distinct opposition groups.

Sometimes candidates are selected long before the actual vacancy occurs, as when a sitting Member informs his supporters of his intention to retire after the next General Election. In this event, the successful applicant, now a fully-fledged "prospective candidate," will be expected to "nurse" the constituency.

This means making oneself agreeable at any public functions which may be held—flower-shows, markets, dinners, dances, and especially functions organized by his own party. My father, when he was "nursing" Marylebone before 1922, used to give up a certain number of evenings to addressing "drawing-room meetings" on political subjects.

When the vacancy has already occurred the machinery is put in motion at once—in the case of a General Election by proclamation, in the case of a by-election by writ or Speaker's warrant. The candidates open their campaign by big inaugural rallies. Usually after this comes the first legal step—nomination.

Nomination is the step which converts our prospective candidate into an official candidate and imposes on him certain rights and liabilities.

With his agent and a few official supporters he visits the returning officer—in my own case the Mayor of Oxford—in the Town Hall with official nomination papers signed by at least two, and probably by many more, constituents, and the sum of £150 in notes or banker's certified draft, which he will receive back if he gets more than an eighth of the votes cast. He is usually snapped by the Press, sheepishly wearing an enormous rosette and shaking hands with his opponent.

He now becomes an official candidate and subject to the full rigours of election law. He must appoint an agent, always in practice the agent employed by the local party association, which under election law dissolves itself for the election, and lets its rooms to the candidate as Committee Rooms. If he decides to act as his own agent (a very foolish act) he must register this also. From now on every penny which is spent in support of his candidature in an election campaign must be recorded as election expenses and returned within a short time of the conclusion of the campaign. Nothing must be spent except by the agent. The election will be invalid if the successful candidate fails to make a return or expends a sum in excess of the maximum allowed—5½d. per elector in boroughs, and 7½d. per elector in counties. Apart from this he must be careful not to treat anyone for anything, but there are no other provisions which usually need worry an honest man.

Who can be selected as a candidate? Any adult British subject, not serving a sentence for crime, bankrupt, mentally afflicted or a member of the House of Lords. No preliminary examination is necessary and no previous experience required. This is right. Democracies must take full responsibility for the people they choose, and quite correctly will not allow their complete freedom of choice to be restricted in any way. A certain number of mistakes are made, but they are fewer than would be expected, and probably fewer than under any other system.

Must a candidate live in his constituency? The rule in America is that he must. But this is found necessary owing to the vast size of the country. It was the rule in England when distances were greater and Parliaments shorter. Now the rule is that this question must be for the electors to determine. In practice borough electors often select an outside man, and county electors usually confine themselves to residents. Constituencies like London or Birmingham are divided into quite arbitrary divisions, and it is comparatively unusual for a member actually to reside within the boundaries. Whatever his origin unless he can afford two houses, the new Member if he gets in will have to live in or near Westminster. The important promise to exact from a candidate is thus not where he will reside, but that he will give a fair share of his time after that which goes to Parliament to constituency affairs.

The campaign is now in full swing. With constituencies of fifty thousand and over it is impossible to conduct a complete personal canvass by the candidate, as was the rule in old days. On the other hand, my own experience has been that nothing brings voters to the poll like a good personal canvass of their neighbours by enthusiastic party workers. Over a campaign of between two to three weeks my calculation is that not more than five thousand separate people usually go to the indoor meetings. If ten thousand hear the candidate once, he is lucky. The regular attendants at meetings are the same people night after night. The value of meetings lies in the fact that the people who go never fail to discuss them with their friends who do not, and nothing gets round quicker than that the candidate has personality, or has none; and nothing cheers supporters like a really good rousing meeting.

This leads me to the subject of heckling and interruption. In my experience a meeting cannot be a first-class success unless there is a certain amount of hostile interruption. In Mr. Gladstone's phrase, public speaking consists in drawing inspiration from the audience in mist and returning it in the form of rain. It is the audience that makes the speech as much as the orator. The ideal audience is a crowd (there is no enthusiasm from an empty hall) three parts in your favour, one-eighth uncertain, and one-eighth vociferously against. Then you can give your best, speaking always to the uncertain, courteous but devastating to your determined opponents, cheered on by your supporters. An audience that is too heavily divided is too restless and heavy for oratory, one solidly for you a bit dull. I have known crowds wholeheartedly against. These are difficult to speak to, because mob psychology is not patient when its mind is made up, and only great courage, great honesty and infinite patience will succeed, and then not always. Eloquence in such circumstances always fails.

I have been talking about heckling—that is *bona fide* interruption by a fair-minded but determined opponent. In my experience this always helps rather than harms the speaker. I am sorry to say that I cannot say the same thing of organized hooliganism, the deliberate drowning of argument by organized shouting and songs. I should like to be able to say that it creates such sympathy that decent people vote against it. That is what they should do—always and irrespective of the complicity of the opposing candidate, because the practice will only be stamped out when it is known not to pay, and that it strikes at the root of government by discussion. But people are not always so strong-minded.

Hooliganism prevents the serious-minded, or the timid, from attending the meetings because they know they will get nothing from them, and prevents those who want to know the arguments from hearing them. It is also extremely physically tiring to the candidate whose nervous and bodily capacity ought to be already taxed to the full if he is giving his best. I personally see no objection to the use of chuckers-out for deliberate hooligans, but the system has been so abused of recent years through its shameful perversion by Fascist thugs and pluguglies, that personally I have never resorted to it. Instead I have used the uniformed police in extreme cases. This means that you can be sure that action is only taken by an independent officer who can be trusted to abstain in all circumstances from violence and has no political bias.

Questions at the end of the meeting are good fun for both sides; I rather doubt if they do much good. The questions are nearly always put by stock question-askers and their hostile character and the sharpness of the repartee which they provoke rather deter the genuine enquirer. Open-air meetings, however, in the main should consist mainly of short statements in answer to questions, especially where no microphone is used since in the main it is not possible to hold the attention of open-air crowds for long periods without a break.

The loud-speaker van is in my opinion the most valuable weapon added to the candidate's armoury in recent years, but the technique is insufficiently appreciated. Inexperienced candidates either try to fire on the move, in which case they descend to foolish and cheap slogans which no one hears and which tend to lower the whole standard of political debate, or they forget that the van is essentially a mobile weapon and use it simply as a means of attracting a small crowd and holding an open-air meeting of the ordinary kind.

This is a mistake. Remember that not more than a tenth of the electorate go to your meetings, and that although your canvass should reach every elector it is not the same thing as the personal touch. The radio van is the instrument which completely baffles the hooligan, which brings Mahomet to the mountain, which should enable every elector to see you or to hear your voice, at least once.

Go into every street in a borough with your radio van. Stop your van. Speak quietly and in a well-moderated microphone. Do not shout and do not orate. On the other hand, aim at speaking for not less than seven or eight minutes. During the first two minutes every window in the street will contain a head. Talk naturally, shortly, sincerely. Give the gist of your case and stop when the heads have begun to go in. No more than two or three speeches for the whole constituency is enough. Do not be afraid of saying the same thing. Try to make sure that every elector knows one reason which you think unanswerable for voting on your side. Do not expect a crowd to collect, and move away when one does. You do not want a public meeting; you are speaking to people in their homes. It is the best alternative to the wireless open to the ordinary candidate.

This brings me to posters and election addresses. I take great trouble with my election address. Do not try to talk down to your constituents. Make it short—not more than fifteen hundred words at most and let it be well printed, with your photograph, a list of your committee rooms, and a list of your meetings. The election address must be addressed and put into envelopes by your keen and devoted supporters. Go and see them as they perform this kind and weary drudgery—the acme of public spirit, and give them a cheery word. The postman will take your address round without a stamp and marked "Election Communication," unless you prefer to save this shot in your locker to answer some last-minute scare on the eve of the poll. In that event you must send your address out by hand.

Posters are essential, but to my mind the elector whose vote will be swayed as the result of seeing your posters is such an ass that he will probably change his mind on the way to the poll. I never use my posters for this purpose. I use them to advertise my meetings and to remind people of their duty, which is to vote. Naturally I ask them to vote for me, but I aim by my poster campaign to remind people who want to support me that this is what they should do. I do not therefore say: "Vote for Hogg and Private Enterprise," or "Vote for Hogg and the Empire," or "Vote for Hogg and more Houses." I have three main posters, one with my

112

photograph, one with "Vote for Hogg," and the other with my meetings. I always keep a shot in my locker against last-minute surprises, and scatter a few Central Office posters of the party leader (they are cheap and do no harm). But in the main I stick to "Vote for Hogg" in large bold type with an additional "to-day" when the time comes. I am assured that on these lines I win my poster campaign.

The national wireless is now available for General Election campaigns, and is in my opinion the most important factor in General Election controversy. Its effect, however, has so far been like that of Hannibal's elephants. With some exceptions it has scattered terror and dismay among the broadcaster's own supporters, and left the enemy in the main unharmed. It has not yet occurred to some of our distinguished statesmen that inept broadcasting, so far from persuading people to vote for them, may actually persuade them to vote against.

This should never happen with any form of propaganda. An advocate may always fail to win a case (one side must lose), but there is no reason at all why he should lose it as the result of what he says himself. The great political chiefs have not yet grasped the essentials of election broadcasting.

The first thing to realize is that people are in their homes and not at public meetings. Half the fun of public meetings is the feeling of comradeship in the psychology of a crowd. The crowd actually seems to tell you what you must say to them. But that is not so in broadcasting. Tricks which are the legitimate and useful apparatus of public oratory are hopelessly out of place—almost obscene—in broadcasting. It is as if an actress wore her stage make-up in the home, or a barrister put on his court voice at the breakfast table or dined in his wig and gown. Phrase-making is less important than a direct, soft, quiet, and above all reasonable manner. It is conversation not oratory, and if you orate into the mike you are not only a bore but a boor. The best thing that can happen is that your listener turns you off before you have made him your permanent enemy.

The next thing to realize is that a party's election broadcasts should not be a series of prize dissertations by public men on general policy. They should be planned on the same principles as those on which any other series of broadcasts should be planned; that is to say, they should be talks by experts setting out stage by stage their own particular viewpoint on particular aspects of policy. That is the only way to make people listen to the series. Show them that you have something definite to say, and show them that if they miss your colleague next Tuesday night when he speaks on economic policy, they will miss something as good but different. The leader should give the lead, and perhaps wind up. So far as possible all reference to the other side should be omitted except for the purpose of defining, as fairly as you can, what the difference is as you see it. Your audience will not listen to what you say about your opponents: they want to hear what you have to say about yourself. They think that is the best way to judge between you.

The campaign ends. Rallies are held on the eve of the poll. On polling day the candidates tour the booths. No more speeches. Good feeling everywhere. It is all over bar the counting, which is attended by candidates, agents, and a number of favoured supporters who check the actual counting of the votes under an oath of secrecy. The votes are sorted, counted into fifties, counted, ballot box by ballot box, at separate tables where sit at least three figures—an official and a checker for each of the two candidates.

The candidate with the most votes wins. This is often attacked as less fair than some system of proportional representation, because it is supposed that a candidate ought not to be elected unless he gets a majority of the votes cast.

It is no part of the purpose of this book to enter into controversial politics. But I must record my view that our present system is the best. I knock out at once many of the systems of proportional representation which depend for their efficacy on having constituencies of seven or eight members, or even more, with party lists from which electors shall choose. I am a convinced believer in the single member system, and anything which tends to modify the principle of one constituency one member even to the extent of restoring two or three member constituencies I should regard as a retrograde step.

This, however, does not answer the main issue. It is possible to combine a certain measure of proportional representation—or at least a second preference vote—with the single member constituency. I believe, however, that the arguments used in favour are based on a fallacy. Democracy in this country [1] should consist

---

[1] I say in this country because where there are racial or religious "minorities" I regard proportional representation as the essential condition of freedom.

in universal suffrage and complete freedom of discussion, but should also be arranged in such a way that the largest organized group should have authority to govern. I believe that democracy will only work if you have strong government. I would rather see my country with a strong government which I thoroughly disapproved of, elected under the present system, than a weak government ineffective, unable to carry out a firm coherent policy in a Parliament in which my own party, together with other groups, was better represented.

I am confirmed in this belief by some of the arguments which are used against me. Weighed up, it nearly always amounts to this: "I want P.R. because it is important to keep Socialism (or Conservatism) out." Alternatively, "I want P.R. because although my own party is the least popular of three or four, I believe that a lot of people would vote for me as the lesser of two evils." I want the electoral system to influence people to direct their minds to the real questions they have to decide, and the real question at a General Election is—which of two or three main teams do I want to govern the country, having regard to practical possibilities?

I do not wish to see teams composed of coalitions of several groups picked up after a Parliament is summoned. Honesty in politics depends on the electors choosing between teams and real issues, not on party groups driving bargains over the heads of the electors when a General Election has failed to produce an intelligible answer because the electors were never compelled to answer one intelligent question.

However, this is a controversial matter, and must be dropped. I end by making a general observation about our system. In America separate elections are held for Senate, House of Representatives and President. Each election is separate and there is no reason why the elector should vote the same ticket in all three. Even if he did, as the system of representation is different in each, it is not only possible but customary for results to differ. In Britain one election serves. In it we decide three cognate but distinct questions. (i) Whom do we wish to see the Member of Parliament for our home town or county? (ii) Whom do we wish to be Prime Minister? (iii) What is the general line of policy we wish to see adopted?

One of the fundamental truths of politics is that nothing is perfect in this world. You may like your candidate but hate his politics, or dislike and fear the leader of his party. It may be that you like the party policy but do not like the candidate. It may be that you like parts of the policy but dislike others. But you cannot pick and choose. You must take all three or reject all three. This is a hard choice. But life is made up of hard choices. There is no clear rule to guide you (although I once invented a "points system" to guide electors). You cannot disregard personal character; you cannot disregard political principle. But under this system you and your consciences are the judges. The people will get the government they deserve.

CHAPTER XV

Basic Procedure

NO writer," says Redlich,[1] "on the historic procedure of the House of Commons can fail to point out its most striking feature—the great antiquity of the forms and rules on which it is based." He goes on to quote two other authorities of great note who make the same point even more specifically.

Palgrave says: "The Parliamentary procedure of 1844 was essentially the procedure on which the House of Commons conducted business during the Long Parliament."

And Porritt[2]: "The most remarkable fact in regard to the procedure of the House is the small change which has taken place since in the reign of Henry VII enactment by Bill superseded enactment by petition."

And, "It is not too much to say that the last House of Commons which met in the Chapel of St. Stephens [3] was following in its main lines the procedure which the journals show to have been in use when in 1547 the House migrated from the Chapter House of Westminster Abbey to the famous Chapel which Edward VI assigned to the Commons."

We have already seen that the history of Parliament falls conveniently into five periods—the mediæval or formative period, the struggle with the Crown, the period of the Unreformed Parliament, the Parliament of the nineteenth century, and the Modern Parliament.

By the end of the mediæval period the salient outlines of the Parliamentary machine and many of the rules of debate already evolved.

Parliament already met in two separate Houses—a step which, it will be remembered, caused the French Estates General some anxious heart searchings at the beginning of the Revolution.

The Commons met, as to-day, under the Presidency of the Speaker who controls the debates and is the formal channel of communication with the other parts of Parliament.

---

[1] Redlich, "Procedure of the House of Commons," Vol. 1.
[2] "The Unreformed House of Commons."
[3] 1834. See Chapter IV, "Where Parliament Meets."

Bills were usually read three times in each House before receiving the Royal Assent. Motions were passed, and Committees appointed, and the Sovereign was always absent from meetings of the House of Commons, and only seldom present in the House of Lords. The basic procedure and rules of debate had already developed the main features which they show to-day.

The debates of the House of Commons and its relations with the other House and the Crown are presided over and controlled by the Speaker of the House of Commons.

In the words of the Manual of Procedure[1]: "The Speaker is (1) the Spokesman and Representative, and (2) the Chairman of the House."

"In the first capacity the Speaker demands the privileges of the House at the beginning of a new Parliament, communicates its resolutions, thanks, censures and admonitions; and issues by its order warrants for the commitment to prison of offenders against its privileges, for the issue of writs to fill vacancies among its members, for the attendance of witnesses, or for bringing prisoners to the bar.

"In the second capacity he presides over the deliberations of the House, maintains order in its debates, decides questions arising on points of order, puts the question for decision, and declares the decision . . .

"The mace is the symbol of the Speaker's authority from the Crown." It follows that when the Speaker is in the Chair, the Mace is on the Table of the House. When the Speaker is not in the Chair because the House is in Committee, the Mace is placed below the table on a bracket. When the House is not in Session, the Mace is removed.

The Speaker is elected at the beginning of each new Parliament by a time-honoured ceremonial which still recalls the day when the office was a dangerous one which might involve the Speaker in conflict with the Crown. He draws a handsome salary (or what the Chancellor allows him to keep of this after deducting income tax) and has an official residence in the Palace of Westminster. His official coach, magnificent in appearance, is said to make the most austere Speaker seasick within ten minutes.

The Speaker is, by a comparatively modern tradition, impartial between the parties, and never now takes part in debates. He possesses a casting vote if the voices are equal. He is assisted by the Chairman of Ways and Means and by the Deputy Chairman

---

[1] S. 23.

who act as Deputy Speaker if for any reason the Speaker is absent from the Chair during the sitting of the House.

On ordinary occasions the Speaker is robed in a black silk gown and a full-bottomed wig similar to that worn ceremonially by judges and K.C.s. His full dress includes a golden robe and lace cuffs and ruffles.

He sits on a raised and canopied chair at one end of the Chamber. Below the Chair is the Table of the House with seats for three Clerks—the Clerk to the House of Commons, and two assistant clerks who sit robed in a short wig and gown.

This arrangement is traditional. In Sir Thomas Smith's words:

"The Speaker sitting in a seat or chair for that purpose somewhat higher that he may see and be seen of them all, hath before him in a lower seat his clerk who readeth such Bills as be first propounded in the lower House or be sent down from the Lords."

The only other official permitted on the floor of the House when the House is sitting is the Sergeant-at-Arms, or his deputy. His function is to maintain order in the lobbies and passages of the House and to execute the orders of the Speaker and of the House. He is armed with a peculiarly ineffective-looking Court sword in a white scabbard, and on the rare occasions when he is called to escort a suspended Member from the Chamber he usually presents a singularly frail and delicate appearance in comparison with the burly politician he is called upon to overawe.

On the right and left of the Speaker are the benches for Members arranged in two blocks on each side with a gangway in the middle —exactly similar to the arrangements for a choir in a church.

Seats cannot be permanently booked, and may be reserved only by the Member himself if he comes in for prayers at the beginning of the day's sitting. But certain seats have come traditionally to carry with them certain implications.

The front seats on the right and left of the Speaker have for many centuries been reserved for persons of Government rank.

The Elizabethan writer Hooker [1] states:

"Upon the lower row on both sides of the Speaker sit such persons as are of the Privy Council or of his chief offices." He adds that no other person had any right to a definite place except the Members for the City of London and those for York which had the ancient privilege of sitting on what is now called the Treasury bench. The Privilege of the Members for the City of London

[1] Quoted Redlich, *op. cit.*, ii. 27.

is acknowledged even now on the first day of each session.

It is a pleasing sight to see the two top-hatted and highly Conservative figures sitting cheek by jowl with the Labour Ministers.

The more modern arrangement of places in which Government and Opposition sit on opposite sides, with ex-Ministers on the "front Opposition bench" is a later development, and is the result of the formation of party and party Government. It was unknown in the seventeenth century; by 1740 it appears to have been well established.

Having thus introduced the House, let us now set the figures in motion. We may note again that the main lines of procedure were already laid down by the end of the mediæval period.

Sir Thomas Smith wrote in 1604: "He that standeth up bare-headed is to be understood that he will speak to the Bill. If more stand up he that is judged first to arise is first heard. Every man speaketh as to the Speaker and not to one another, for that is against the order of the House."

This does not differ greatly from the present Manual of Procedure:

"A Member who desires to speak must rise in his place uncovered and address himself to the Speaker. . . . When a Member rises to speak, his name is called by the Speaker. . . . If more Members than one rise at the same time, the Member whose name is so called is entitled to speak."

Theoretically all Members of the House are equal, and none has a prior right to speak over any other. "A principle which is especially distinctive of English Parliamentary life, is the protection of the minority as a fundamental basis of Parliamentary Government. . . . Complete equality of all members is the venerable and immovable basis of all procedure both in theory and practice and the legal foundation of all Parliamentary action."

This equally appears at the outset in the right to speak in the House. No one can speak as of right—but only "if he catches the Speaker's eye." The Speaker cannot prevent anyone from speaking if there is time, and no one else desires to do so—but as in any important matter time is limited and would-be orators numerous— the whole course of debate is altered according to the Speaker's absolute discretion. By custom, no one is permitted to question this discretion, and the Speaker is always reticent in justifying particular decisions by giving reasons.

This wise reserve is the essence of the whole matter. The

Speaker's business is to give the best, fullest and freest discussion that time and circumstances permit. Many are disappointed, and there is no rule, as in America, that undelivered speeches may none the less be recorded in the official report.

Certain general observations regarding the Speaker's use of his discretion begin to dawn on the Member of Parliament after some years. Important discussions usually begin and end by speeches from the Government or Opposition front benches, and informal agreements take place as to the times when these begin and end.

The Speaker is usually indulgent to Members who speak for the first time and calls them in preference to more seasoned speakers, who have to wait their turn with congratulations on their lips for the "maiden" who has deprived them of their place.

It has sometimes been observed that those who are called during the dinner hour are not always the most scintillating orators, and that when tempers begin to rise, the calling of a dull speaker sometimes conveniently cools the air.

Unlike many continental assemblies, once a speaker is "on his feet" the House is at his mercy. There is no time limit, but it has been noticed that orators who outstay their welcome sometimes find it rather more difficult to attract the Speaker's eye in spite of plaintive cries of "Mr. Speaker" on another occasion.

As befits a place where matters which arouse the deepest feeling are discussed, the most formal conventions have long attended the actual words and phrases which may or may not be used.

The most fundamental of these is the rule that only the Speaker may utter a Member's name, and, except where he calls upon him to speak, even this is only done by way of solemn reproof after serious warning.

To quote Sir Thomas Smith again: "It is also taken against the order to name him who you do not confute but by circumlocution as 'he that speaketh with the Bill,' or 'he that spake against the Bill,' or 'gave this or that reason.' "

This fundamental principle had by the end of the eighteenth century crystallized into certain formal conventions. Thus all Members, especially political opponents, are "honourable" unless they are privy councillors when they are "right honourable" or holders of Irish peerages or courtesy titles when they are "noble." All Members who are of His Majesty's counsel are "honourable and learned," and all who hold His Majesty's Commission "honourable and gallant." An opponent is an "honourable gentleman," a Member of the same party is an "honourable friend." Formal courtesy is by no means the least necessary arm to assist government by discussion.

Beyond this, extreme care is used not to impute motives or to use "unparliamentary" language. "No reviling or nipping words must be used," says Sir Thomas Smith, once again as usual up-to-date, "for then all the House will cry 'It is against the order.' " In the words of the Manual of Procedure: "A Member while speaking on a question must not refer to any other Member by his name nor make a personal charge against any Member."

Under this rule any charge of lying or the like is wholly out of order and, if the Speaker hears it, a Member making such a charge will be made to withdraw it. It is sometimes thought that this rule is more honoured in the breach than in the observance, and certain time-honoured chestnuts are told about the ways in which it can be disregarded.

The most famous of these, perhaps, is Mr. Winston Churchill's phrase "a terminological inexactitude." An Irish Member is alleged to have said, "I may not call the honourable gentleman a liar, but I will say that if I saw him walking across Waterloo Bridge with Ananias on one side and Sapphira on the other, I should say he was keeping very suitable company"; but perhaps he was not heard by the Speaker of the day. My own experience has been that personal charges, quite apart from the rules of order which are usually honourably kept, are best left alone, or if made are best withdrawn, quite irrespective of any direction from the Chair.

Other basic rules of procedure which were fully established by the end of the mediæval period were the rule against speaking twice (except in Committee), the main procedure on a Bill, and the method of taking the vote.

Voting in the House of Commons is primarily by voice. Every matter which occasions discussion in the House, apart from personal statements, and questions to Ministers, can only take place if there is a question before the House. This may be a resolution, or it may be "that this House do now adjourn," or "that this Bill be read a second time," or, more complicated, "that the words proposed to be left out stand part of the motion," but in every case there must be a question capable of the answer "yes" or "no." In the words of an early Standing Order of 1604, "Ordered, that nothing do pass by order of the House without a question; and that no order without a question affirmative or negative."

When discussion is complete, Sir Thomas Smith observed, "The Speaker sayth as many will have this Bill go forward say 'yea.' Then they which allow the Bill crie 'yea,' and any who will not say 'no.' As the crie of 'yea' or 'no' is bigger, so the Bill is allowed or dashed."

Probably nine questions out of ten to this day are settled by the voices. The formula now used is almost identical with that recorded by Sir Thomas Smith. The Speaker says: "The question is that this Bill be read a second time. As many as are of that opinion say 'Aye' (AYE!), to the contrary 'no' (NO!), I think the AYES have it (NO!!!)."

If the Noes persist with their opposition, the House proceeds to a division. In Sir Thomas Smith's words, "If it be a doubt which crie is the bigger they divide the House." In Sir Thomas Smith's day and until 1834, the division took place by the Ayes leaving the Chamber and being counted as they left it, and the Noes remaining inside and being counted in their places. This, of course, gave an advantage to the Noes, who numbered the idle amongst their adherents. The struggle to get the question put in such a way as to make one side 'no' still has left marks on certain points of our procedure.

The present method of division, though essentially the same, has three refinements.

(1) Both sides must leave the Chamber and pass through lobbies running adjacent to the House, the 'aye' lobby on the Speaker's right and the 'no' lobby on his left.

(2) Both sides appoint two tellers, one for each lobby and one of these counts and the other checks Members as they emerge from the partly-closed doors of the lobby with a little formal bow.

(3) Before they reach the exits of the lobby their names are checked by some of the clerks of the House who prepare the official "division list" which is printed with the votes and proceedings and in *Hansard*.

When the voting is complete the votes are recorded on a card, and the tellers form up in front of the table, the winning side on the right. One of the winning tellers reads out the figures, bows, and hands the card to the Chair. The Speaker then formally announces the result as follows:—

The "Ayes" to the right were ..	345
The "Noes" to the left were ..	196
so the Ayes have it."	

CHAPTER XVI

Question Time

THE first hour of the House of Commons' time for the first four days of the week is taken up with questions, and in addition to the questions which are put down for oral answer during this hour, there are numerous others in which only a written reply is circulated in the official report. Question time in the House of Commons is perhaps the most characteristic and one of the most valuable features of modern procedure. It is the one occasion when the private Member can still of his own initiative and without much restriction inaugurate any subject for momentary discussion by the House of Commons, almost the one occasion when the House seems to reappear in its traditional rôle of the champion of the individual against the executive, and the private Member appears as the equal or even the superior of the occupants of the front benches. It has been said, that question time "throws a searchlight upon every corner of the public service." The object of questions is "the explanation to the public of the meaning of political events." They are even "often arranged by the government itself so as to give them an opportunity of making announcements in a somewhat informal way."

The institution of questions, and particularly of question time is of comparatively recent origin. The first recorded question was put in the House of Lords in 1721. The first printed notice of questions was issued in 1835. By 1847 the number of questions to Ministers numbered one a day; by 1880 there were 1,546 during the session, or about 13 a day. But from this point the increase was much more dramatic. In 1900 the average had grown to 41 per day, and by 1902 the number which any one Member could ask in a day was rationed. At one time the ration was six, but in 1930 the daily quota per Member was reduced to three—the figure at which it still stands. On this ration there are in peace-time over one hundred questions a day for oral answer, not counting those for written answer.

The explanation of this remarkable growth is of course in part the gradual encroachment of the time of private Members by the executive; in the main, however, the vast increase in the complexity of the modern administrative machine renders the short question and answer the only practicable way in which Parliament can retain any reasonable hope of scrutinizing the action of the executive.

How are questions asked? The first stage is for the Member who wishes to ask a question to write it down and to hand it in to one of the clerks at the table with his name and if he wants an oral answer asterisk. Thus:—

* Mr. Buggins: To ask the Postmaster-General how many picture postcards were delivered to old ladies over seventy on Christmas Day, 1945.

It is the business of the Clerk at the table to make sure that Mr. Buggins' question is in order. For this purpose he applies the following rules:

(i) The question must relate to that branch of public affairs for which the Minister is responsible. For this reason there are certain matters—notably the matter of the Home Programmes of the B.B.C.—which are difficult or impossible to raise at question time.

(ii) A question must not publish any name or statement not strictly necessary to make the question intelligible.

(iii) If a question contains a statement the Member asking it must make himself responsible for the accuracy of the statement. This means amongst other things that you cannot put down questions based on a newspaper report unless you are prepared yourself to make yourself responsible to the extent of any allegation of fact contained in the question.

(iv) A question must not contain any argument, inference, imputation, epithet, or ironical expression.

(v) A question must not refer to any debate that has occurred or answer that has been given in the current session.

(vi) A question must not be asked about proceedings in a committee which has not reported.

(vii) A question must not ask for an expression of opinion, or for the solution of an abstract legal question or of a hypothetical proposition.

(viii) A question may not be asked as to the character or conduct of any person except in his official or public capacity.

(ix) There are certain persons—the heir to the throne, the Viceroy of India and the Governors-General of the Dominions, High Court and County Court judges (or persons in equivalent positions), the Lord Chancellor, the Speaker or Members of either

House of Parliament, whose conduct may not be impugned by question or in debate but only by a substantive motion on the order paper.

(x) A question conveying a personal charge may be disallowed.

(xi) A question once fully answered may not be asked again.

Questions may be asked of any Minister, or of a private Member if it relates to some matter connected with the business of the House for which the Member is responsible. The only private Members normally asked questions in the last Parliament were the Chairman of the Kitchen Committee, and Sir G. Courthope as a Forestry Commissioner.

There are always, on any given day, more questions asked than can possibly be answered in the hour available. The practice has therefore arisen of arranging an elaborate series of priorities whereby the questions for each department take it in turns to come up first on any particular day. Even so, some departments remain low on the list.

Mr. Buggins will be told that the first day on which the questions for the Postmaster-General will come early on the list is next Thursday.

The Clerk to the Table arranges that the questions handed in each day are printed on the Order Paper. In this way the Minister receives notice of the question which he is to be asked.

The machinery of the Civil Service is then set to work at full pressure to answer the question in time. The practice of different departments differs, but in each case the question is cut out of the Order Paper, pasted on a clean slip and put inside a distinctively-coloured folder with the highest priority marking and entitled Parliamentary Questions for answer—immediate, together with the most elaborate instructions for clearing the file in the most expeditious way.

The folders containing the questions for next Thursday (including Mr. Buggins') will now start circulating within the Ministry at top speed. It will go from subordinate to superior, from section to section of the Ministry until all the officials who are or might be interested have had their say and a draft answer has been prepared.

This draft answer will be submitted to the Minister and settled by him personally—either in accordance with the terms of the draft or in terms he drafts himself.

Beneath the actual answer to be delivered a series of remarks entitled "Notes for Minister," or as the case may be, generally appears.

These contain the information which it is thought likely the Minister will find useful in answering any supplementary questions.

On Thursday afternoon the Minister appears with his bundle of coloured folders on his seat on the Treasury bench.

Questions are taken immediately after private business (if any), and when the time for asking them arrives the Speaker calls successively each Member in whose name a question appears on the Order Paper.

Mr. Buggins is number 13, and when his name is called, Mr. Buggins rises in his place and says:

"Number thirteen, sir. Of the Postmaster-General," and the Postmaster-General delivers his prepared answer.

Now is the time for supplementaries. The Speaker normally calls the asker of the original question, if he cares to ask one. Mr. Buggins has one ready and is already on his feet.

"Can the Right Honourable Gentleman explain why the figures for 1945 show such a startling increase over the figures for 1944?"

This is one of the questions anticipated by the Civil Service, and the answer comes back as smooth as butter.

The game is now open. The Speaker will probably allow one or more questions from other Members who are interested. One of these is Mr. Stiggins, who believes in free postage for old age pensioners. He has already marked the question down as an occasion for trotting out his hobby and his plaintive cries of "Mr. Speaker" began to be heard almost before the original answer was out of the Minister's mouth. The Speaker is kind, and calls Mr. Stiggins, who asks:

"Is not the Right Honourable Gentleman aware that the provision of free postage for old age pensioners would greatly increase this most desirable form of traffic?"

The Speaker hesitates whether to rule this question out as not arising from the original answer. The Minister hesitates as to whether to say "I must have notice of that," decides against it, and considers that he can take this in his stride. "I am aware," he replies, "that in the present circumstances and shortage of man power the post office workers have already enough to do without increasing the traffic by any concessions of free postage."

The Speaker decides that the House has had enough of it and calls the next question.

Before the war it sometimes happened that the list of questions was completed before the hour allotted for question time was over. In this event the Speaker went through the list a second time calling any question which owing either to the absence of the Member who asked it or of the Minister who was to answer had been missed out. On the "second time round" a question could be put by a Member other than he who had put the question down.

Nowadays the list is seldom if ever finished. Questions which are not asked owing to the absence of a Member, and questions which are not reached are treated as questions for written answer and the replies circulated in *Hansard*—the only instance in British practice of the Official Report containing matter intended to be but not in fact delivered in the House.

If a Member is not satisfied with the answer he receives to a question he may raise the matter on the adjournment.[1] In practice most of the subjects which are selected for the "half-hour adjournment" debates are those which have been previously raised at question time. A dissatisfied Member usually, but not always gives notice of his intention at the time of receiving the reply by saying:

"To a point of order, Mr. Speaker, I beg to give notice that owing to the unsatisfactory nature of the reply I will raise this matter on the Adjournment." He then proceeds by appointment to the Speaker's secretary who tells him whether any of the "half-hour Adjournments" in the next fortnight are, in fact, free.

After the time for questions is at an end the Speaker may have given leave—in cases of sufficient urgency and importance—to a Member to ask a question of which he has given private notice. In this event he has probably handed a manuscript question to the Speaker the night before and taken steps to see that the Minister is informed of its contents and his intention to ask it. A serious explosion or railway accident—or some public event of outstanding importance requiring an immediate answer may be the subject of a private notice question. The Speaker is usually extremely careful only to permit this privilege in cases which clearly call for it—if notice of a similar question is already on the Order Paper he will in no case allow it.

After question time is also the occasion for Ministerial Statements, and private explanations or apologies.

If a Minister considers it desirable to make a public announce-

[1] See p. 140 ff.

ment of policy in advance of any debate on the subject he will usually take advantage of this privilege. Announcements of forth-coming international policy—changes in the rate of war pensions, and other matters considered important enough to be disclosed in this way but not calling for debate are frequently dealt with in this way. On such occasions questions, on the lines of supplementary questions, can be asked, but no debate can arise.

Personal explanations are permitted at this time "by the indulgence of the House." The most regular occasion for such a personal explanation is the resignation of a Minister who takes the opportunity, from a seat on the back benches, to explain in as uncontroversial a manner as possible the circumstances which have given rise to his resignation. But other occasions, though less conforming to a pattern, are more frequent. There are many occasions when a Member may find that his public conduct has been misrepresented, or has occasioned need for explanation or apology, and the House is generally indulgent to Members who reasonably use this concession. The most recent case was where a Member of the Labour Party had inadvertently attributed a speech she was attacking to the wrong Conservative Member who held views quite different from the Member who had made the speech. But no general rule can be given. On other occasions Members raising questions of privilege, Members seeking the Speaker's guidance, or Members who desired to apologize for unseemly behaviour have spoken at this time.

On Thursdays after question time the Leader of the Opposition by custom asks the Leader of the House to state the Business for next week.

The whole time of the House is now given over to government business, and this "business question" is therefore the only occasion in which Members can publicly question the propriety with which the Government has used their rights. The answer to the "business question" usually provokes ten or fifteen minutes of supplementary question and answer. Apart from this, questions of suitable subjects for debate are discussed in private through what are called "the usual channels," which in the case of Government and Official Oppositions means the party whips.

CHAPTER XVII

The Passing of a Bill

STATUTES originated in the practice whereby the two Houses petitioned the Crown. It was then the King's business to allow or refuse such petitions, and if he allowed them they were then recorded in suitable form on the Statute Rolls when Parliament had dispersed.

This procedure gave rise to constant complaint for the very good reason that what found its way on to the Statute Roll differed widely from the terms of the petition. Thus we read in 1414: "The King of his grace especial graunteth that fro hensforth nothing be enacted to the peticions of his commons that be contrarie of their askynge whereby they should be bounden without their assent."

Under Henry V and Henry VI it gradually came to be established practice that Statutes should be enacted by Bill and not by the King as result of petition.

A Bill is a draft Act of Parliament which the King has to accept in whole or reject in whole. Since the reign of Queen Anne the formula of rejection (Le Roy s'avisera) has never been used.

The passing of Bills is one of the main functions of Parliament, and the procedure is extremely ancient.

A Bill normally consists of the following parts:—

(1) A long title which describes the various purposes for which legislation is desired.

(2) A short title which is the name by which it is generally known.

(3) A preamble which may contain a number of assertions about the desirability of legislating on the particular subject (this part is now often omitted) concluding with the words, in the case of a non-financial Bill:

"Be it enacted by the King's Most Excellent Majesty, by and with the advice and consent of the Lords Spiritual and Temporal and Commons in this present Parliament assembled and by the authority of the same, as follows." Then follow:

(4) The clauses of the Bill (which become "sections" when the Bill becomes an Act) containing the main provisions. The sections are followed:

(5) By the Schedules which usually contain lists—such as lists of Statutes repealed or amended, and details of machinery or procedure rendered necessary by the main provisions of the Bill.

(6) When the Bill receives the Royal Assent, but not before the Bill receives a serial number of its own which shows the session in which it was passed and the position occupied by the Bill among other Acts passed during the session. To give a random example, the Herring Industry Act, 1944, was given the serial description 7 & 8 Geo. VI c. 32, which means the thirty-second Act (or "Chapter") passed in the session which occupied parts of the seventh and eighth years of the reign of King George the Sixth. Some old Acts were known solely by this description, but it is not clear what advantage is obtained by continuing the practice now.

A good instance of most of these features of an Act of Parliament is the Parliament Act, 1911.

The serial number of the Act is 1 & 2 Geo. V c. 11, because it was the eleventh Act passed in the Session of Parliament which took place during the first and second years of the reign of King George the Fifth.

The long title of the Act is "An Act to make provision with respect to the powers of the House of Lords in relation to those of the House of Commons and to limit the duration of Parliament." The last phrase was necessary because in addition to curtailing the powers of the House of Lords the Act amended the Septennial Act, 1715, so as to make the maximum length of a Parliament five instead of seven years.

The short title of the Act contained in section 8 is "The Parliament Act, 1911."

The Preamble to the Act reads as follows:—

"Whereas it is expedient that provision should be made for regulating the relations between the two Houses of Parliament, and whereas it is intended to substitute for the House of Lords as it at present exists a Second Chamber constituted on a popular instead of on an hereditary basis, but such substitution cannot be brought immediately into operation:

And whereas provision will require hereafter to be made by Parliament in a measure effecting such substitution for limiting and defining the powers of the new Second Chamber, but it is expedient to make such provisions as in this Act appears for restricting the existing powers of the House of Lords:

Be it therefore enacted by the King's Most Excellent Majesty, by and with the advice and consent of the Lords Spiritual and Temporal, and Commons in this present Parliament assembled, and by the authority of the same as follows:"

This preamble well illustrates the unwisdom of preambles. Let an Act speak for itself. It had better not prophesy.

There are no schedules to the Parliament Act, 1911. In this it may be called blessed.

Bills are of three main types—Public, Private, and Hybrid.

A Public Bill has as its object an alteration in the general law.

A Private Bill is a Bill which has as its object an alteration in the law relating to some particular locality or to confer rights on or relieve from liability some particular person or bodies of persons. At present Private Bills are brought in usually at the request of a local authority. But a Private Bill is the last resort of any subject who cannot achieve what he regards as his rights by any known process of law. Up to 1857 it was the only method of divorce known to the law of the land, and divorces are still given by Act of Parliament in Northern Ireland.

A Hybrid Bill is a Public Bill which nonetheless affects private interests in such a way that the Private Bill procedure is in some respects more appropriate. The Bill under which the nationalization of the Bank of England was achieved was dealt with as a Hybrid Bill, because the nationalization procedure necessarily affected the rights of individual shareholders who were bought out by the terms of the Bill itself. The Bill nationalizing the Coal Mines is not a Hybrid Bill because the clauses affecting the ownership of the assets to be transferred set up a tribunal machinery to deal with claims and compensation outside the provisions of the Bill itself.

The procedure on Private Bills is complicated, and differs in many aspects from that of Public Bills. The details, however, are unimportant. The basic differences are that (i) the effective discussions on Private Bills do not take place on the floor of the House but in Select Committees, and (ii) that proceedings in the Select Committees are conducted in a manner which resembles contentious litigation in front of a court rather than legislation before a Parliament. Speeches are made by interested parties, who are not Members of the House, Counsel appear, witnesses are called, and evidence given. Enormous trouble is taken to "prove the preamble" by evidence before the Committee. The procedure on the floor of the House is usually formal, and where opposed is only usually debated on the floor of the House on some public ground. The last Private Bill to be opposed on the floor of the House was a Railway Bill which was opposed by the railway clerks' trade union in order to make a grievance against the Company effective.

What follows in this chapter is an account on the procedure on Public Bills only.

Bills other than Money Bills originate in either House of Parliament. For convenience' sake the assumption will be made in what follows that the Bill we are following has been introduced into the House of Commons. This is the case with nearly all major Government measures, and even where the Bill originates in the Lords, the differences in procedure are all merely consequential.

When an assembly has before it a complex draft which it must accept or reject with or without amendment the modern practice is to circulate a printed draft in advance and to have the printed draft in front of the meeting at the time.

This, of course, is the practice with Bills in Parliament, but the stages through which it passes through both Houses in order to become law bear clear vestiges of an older usage. Before the printing press—perhaps before it could be treated as absolutely certain that knights and burgesses or even noble lords could read, it would be natural that Bills intended to be passed should be read from the Chair. Whether this be the explanation or not, the three main milestones in the passage of a Bill through each House are called the three readings of the Bill. In fact, of course, the Bill is not read publicly at all, and the phrase "reading" is now no more than a relic; even the debates on the three readings do not now quite accurately mark the substantial stages of the procedure.

That a Bill should pass three readings was already the normal practice before the death of Queen Elizabeth. Sir Thomas Smith records: "All Bills be thrice, on three diverse days read and disputed upon before they come to the question."

As a matter of fact this was still not an absolutely invariable practice. As late as 1628 the Petition of Right passed through the House of Commons by a different procedure after only a single reading.

Until comparatively recently a Public Bill was introduced into the House of Commons on a resolution being passed giving leave to introduce the Bill, and at one time the first reading of the Bill which followed was sometimes the occasion of debate and opposition.

At present, however, a Bill can be brought in without leave; the first reading is given without debate and is in effect only an order for printing and publishing the Bill.

The effective stages in the passage of a Public Bill, other than a Money Bill, at the present day are:—

Second Reading.
Committee.
Report.
Third Reading.

Although the right of private Members to introduce Bills has never been formally abolished, it had already fallen into decay in the days before the war of 1939, and since 1939 has been in abeyance owing to the seizure by the Government of all Parliamentary time in the House of Commons for their own use. A Private Member of the House of Lords could still introduce a Bill in the Upper House—but as it could not receive any time for discussion in the House of Commons without Government support this right must be considered nugatory,[1] For practical purposes at the present time only Government Bills can be introduced into Parliament.

The first main occasion for the debate of a modern Bill is therefore the Second Reading. On this occasion the debate is limited to a discussion of the principles of the Bill. Detailed discussion including criticism which could be met by minor alterations is reserved for the Committee or Report Stages.

On the occasion of the Second Reading debate the motion is "That this Bill be now read a second time," and critics who wish to secure the rejection of the Bill may take any one of three courses. In the first place they may simply vote against the motion and leave it to their speeches to explain their reasons. A more picturesque manner of doing the same thing is by putting down an amendment to omit the word "now" from the motion and adding at the end "on this day six months." A more common course, however, is to put down what is called a "reasoned rejection." This is in the form of an amendment to omit "all after that" and to insert some suitable words giving the reasons which animate opponents to the Bill in carrying their opposition into the division lobby. A reasoned motion for the rejection of a Bill on

---

[1] Since writing this I have learned that a private Members' Bill has been introduced into the Upper House. If it becomes an Act, I shall have been wrong.

second reading might therefore read "Leave out all after 'that' and insert 'this' House, while recognizing the urgent necessity for legislation providing for the adequate housing of the people, nevertheless declines to give a second reading to a Bill which ignores the contribution which might be made to this object by private enterprise (or local authorities), which relies upon the discredited theory of subsidies (or which fails to apply the well-tried and successful method of granting subsidies in respect of completed houses), and which can only succeed in the long run in raising the cost of housing without in any way increasing the supply of dwelling-houses of an adequate standard to serve as homes for the people."

When a Public Bill has passed its Second Reading it is then ordered to be committed either to a "Committee of the whole House" or to one of the regular Standing Committees formed for the purpose.

The Committee of the whole House was originally a device framed probably in the reign of James I for the purpose of conducting debates in which the Speaker, usually a nominee of the Crown, was not in the Chair. As a method of procedure it has had many vicissitudes, and we shall meet it again when we deal with financial matters. At present, under the Standing Orders and practice introduced by the present Labour Government, it is normally used for discussing only those Bills which are of the highest constitutional importance, or those in which the Committee stage is likely to be a pure formality.

In all other cases Bills are committed to a Standing Committee. Under the present rules these are at present five in number,[1] and apart from the Scottish Committee consist of a nucleus of twenty members with up to twenty members added as being particularly suitable for the Bill in question. The Standing Committees are held in the Committee-rooms on the upper floors of the House, and normally sit at 10.30 in the morning on two days a week. It is unusual and considered generally undesirable for a Standing Committee to sit during the time allotted for sittings of the House of Commons. The Standing Committees are presided over by a member of the Speaker's panel of at least ten temporary chairmen.

Proceedings in Committee, are in general modelled on those of the House of Commons itself, with the solitary important excep-

---

[1] Committees A, B, C and D, and the Scottish Grand Committee. There is power to increase the number as necessary.

tion that Members may speak twice in the same debate. In Committee of the whole House the Speaker's Chair is left empty, and the Mace is on the bracket under the table. The Chairman sits in the lower chair normally reserved for the Clerk of the House. It is the practice in Committee to address the Chairman by his name, and not as "Mr. Chairman" or "Mr. Deputy Chairman."

The object of the Committee stage in the Bill is the amendment of its individual provisions, and any amendment can be proposed in Committee if it is relevant to the subject-matter of the Bill and within the scope of the title of the Bill. If relevant to the subject-matter but outside the scope of the title, the title itself must be amended and the Committee makes a special report to the House.

The order in which the several parts of a Bill are dealt with in Committee is:—

    (i) The clauses in order.
    (ii) Proposed new clauses, if any.
    (iii) Schedules.
    (iv) Proposed new schedules, if any.
    (v) The Preamble.
    (vi) The Title.

Any Member may propose amendments to the Bill on the Committee stage. An amendment may take the form of an omission, an addition, or a substitution of words in the Bill, or of a totally new clause.

Each amendment has to be framed in such a way that it can be put in the form of a "question" or a series of questions on which Members may vote "aye" or "no."

Thus, where the nature of an amendment is that of a substitution of words, the amendment is put down on the Order Paper by its mover in the following form:—

    "Page 9, clause 8, line 11, leave out 'and' and insert 'where by reason of.' "

And when the Chairman comes to put the question, he puts two questions to the Committee. The first question is not, as one might suppose, that the word 'and' be left out of the clause. It is the other way round. The Chairman says: "The question I have to put is 'that the word "and" stand part of the clause.' "

The origin of this peculiarity of procedure is obscure, but it is believed to have been due to the disputes which used to develop under the old method of voting [1] which gave an advantage to the "noes" over the "ayes."

The second question, which is only put if the "noes" have it on the first, is "that the words 'where by reason of' be there inserted." The supporters of the amendment will thus vote "no" on the first question and "aye" on the second. This accounts for the fact that Members, who may know quite well what they want to achieve, sometimes find it quite hard to remember in which particular lobby they should record their vote in order to achieve it.

Where the order paper contains no amendments on a particular clause, or where the amendments are all disposed of, the Chairman calls the number of the clause and a discussion takes place about the clause as a whole on the question that "clause Eight or clause Eight as amended (as the case may be) stand part of the Bill." This discussion is clearly wider than on any particular amendment and gives an opportunity of discussing both the principle of the clause, the relation of the clause to the Bill, together with the general consequences of any amendments which have been carried.

Where an amendment takes the form of a new clause altogether, the consideration of this, whatever its ultimate place will be in the Bill when it becomes an Act, is postponed until the other clauses have been disposed of. It must then first be given a "second reading" by the Committee. It is then open to be amended like any other clause, and a final discussion takes place on the question "that the clause, or the clause as amended, be added to the Bill."

After the clauses, the schedules, and any new schedules are taken in the same way, and after the schedules, the preamble, and finally after the preamble the title, which may have to be amended in view of new clauses adding to or modifying the scope of the Bill.

Finally the Chairman puts the last question, "That I report the Bill as amended to the House," and this, if agreed to, brings the Committee stage to an end.

In Committee of the whole House, but not in Standing Committee, proceedings may be interrupted by a motion that the Chairman report progress and ask leave to sit again. This motion is made when it appears that the discussion has reached a stage when further proceedings would be useless for the time being.

[1] See p. 123.

It may be moved on behalf of the Government when it desires time to consider important concessions, or by the Opposition if they feel that the Government is not giving adequate attention to a particular point of view. It is within the discretion of the Chair to refuse to accept this motion if moved. The comparable procedure on Standing Committee is a motion for the adjournment of the Debate.

When it has passed Committee, a Bill has still to receive consideration in two more stages in the whole House.

The first of these is the Report Stage, and the second is Third Reading. The object of the Report Stage is to give the whole House an opportunity of considering the details of a Bill or for any further amendments to be introduced. The procedure is in form almost a reproduction of the Committee proceedings, except that proposed new clauses are discussed before proposed amendments. However, the Chair has very drastic powers to circumscribe the report stage by refusing to call any amendments considered of insufficient importance or on which there has been adequate discussion on Committee.

On the Report Stage of a Bill the House may recommit it in whole or in part to a Committee. If it passes the Report Stage without this course being taken, it then reaches its final stage, or Third Reading, before being sent to the Upper House. On this Third Reading it is still possible to make verbal amendments or an amendment to the title of the Bill, but such amendments are rare, and the Third Reading debate ranges mainly on general principles, or on the refusal by the Government of particular concessions or amendments. Originally the Third Reading was followed by a motion that the Bill do pass. This further stage is now omitted in the Commons, although retained in the Lords. If the Bill passes its Third Reading in the Commons, an order is automatically made that the Clerk of the House carry the Bill to the Lords and desire their concurrence.

The Bill has now to pass a similar number of stages in the Upper House. It is unnecessary to recount the various minor points in which the procedure differs; in general, it is on the same lines.

If the Lords amend the Bill, a further discussion must take place in the Commons "on consideration of the Lords' amendments." On each amendment a resolution is passed "That this House doth agree (or disagree) with the Lords in the said amendment." If there is no disagreement, the Bill is now ready for the Royal Assent. This is the normal course of events.

Procedure still exists, however, whereby the House of Commons may insist that the Lords' amendments be rejected, and if in relation to a particular amendment the motion of disagreement is passed, a Committee to draw up reasons to be assigned to the Lords for the disagreement is set up, and a message to the Lords embodying the reasons is sent. The Lords may then reamend the Bill to conform with the view of the Commons, make proposals for alternative amendments, or insist on their original amendments. In this event the Commons may agree with the Lords, make counter-proposals of their own, withdraw the Bill altogether, or, in theory, demand a conference. The last procedure may now be regarded as obsolete, since in the event of a real disagreement arising, the Government of the day would certainly, if they regarded the matter as of sufficient importance, apply the Parliament Act Procedure, or even, perhaps, employ the Royal Prerogative to create new peers.[1]

The Bill is now ready for the Royal Assent which, as described elsewhere in this volume is given, usually to batches of Bills, but sometimes to single measures, in Norman French in the House of Lords.

Since the reign of Queen Victoria the sovereign has never performed this routine duty in person. A Commission under the Great Seal appoints certain distinguished persons to act as Lords Commissioners, and in their presence the Clerk of the Parliament reads out the titles of the bills to be passed, and after each the appropriate formula in Norman French, which varies slightly according as to whether the new Act is a Private Act, a Public Act, or an Act granting supply. When this is done the new law finds its place on the Statute Book as an Act of Parliament.

---

[1] See p. 29.

CHAPTER XVIII

The Humble Address, The Adjournment and on Resolutions

EVERY Parliament and every session of Parliament is opened by a speech from the Throne delivered in the House of Lords, either by the King in person or by a Royal Commission under the Great Seal.

This Speech (which in origin and form contains the King's request from Parliament for legislation and supply), contains the Government's programme of work for Parliament for the ensuing year. It is customary for Commons and Lords to give considered replies to the Royal demands in the form of a humble address.

The "Debate on the Address" is therefore usually the first controversial business at the beginning of each Parliament. The terms of the Address are in formal terms, expressing thanks for the gracious speech, and it is the practice of the Government to enlist the support of two relatively junior private Members to move it and second it on the first effective day of the sittings after formal business. Thereafter a wide debate, for which several days are normally given, takes place on the whole of the Government's programme for the year. It is a frequent practice for Members to propose amendments which usually take the form of adding to the expression of humble thanks the words "but regrets" and a suitable expression of censure at the errors of commission or omission exhibited by the Speech. After a general debate of some days, the Speaker usually narrows the discussion to one or more topics by calling one or more of these amendments.

The debate on the Adjournment derives its form from the struggle between Crown and Parliament, dramatically symbolized by the incident in which the Speaker was held down in his chair until the essential business of the House was carried through.

The theory on which the Adjournment debate was based is that the House shall not adjourn until all manner of grievances have been fully ventilated. It follows that when the motion is proposed that this House do now adjourn, a Member who catches the Speaker's eye is permitted to discuss almost any subject he desires that does not involve legislation.

At the present time the Adjournment debate is used in the main on four separate types of occasion:—

(i) General debates inaugurated by the Government for their own purposes in their own time;

(ii) debates inaugurated by critics of the Government on a "definite matter of public importance";

(iii) debates at the end of a sitting before the House goes into recess; and

(iv) the daily "half-hour Adjournment" at the end of the day's debate.

General debates on the Adjournment take place on the initiative of the Government without much limitation—except the general rule forbidding the discussion of matters requiring legislation and the inevitably indecisive conclusion of such debates.

The right to secure a debate on the Adjournment to discuss a "definite matter of urgent public importance" is so heavily circumscribed with formality that an attempt to bring about such a debate scarcely ever succeeds. Even if the motion passes the Speaker's eagle scrutiny, it is necessary to have the support of not less than forty Members or win the right of a debate on a division.

The Adjournment at the end of every sitting, before the House goes into recess, is a customary concession by the Government who usually give a whole day for the purpose. Although the subject is of course in theory unlimited, the actual subjects discussed and the times allotted to each are usually prearranged informally by agreement between the party whips, the Speaker, and any individual concerned.

The "half-hour Adjournment" is a facility for public discussion of minor grievances which has developed greatly in the past three or four years owing to a number of causes. These include:—

(i) The earlier hour at which debates normally terminate, which renders a Press report of the Adjournment debate at the end a practical proposition.

(ii) The increased pressure on Parliamentary time, resulting in the curtailment of private Members' rights in other directions.

(iii) The vastly increased complication in the administrative machine resulting in a greatly increased number of individual grievances, with a short public debate of half an hour in the House of Commons, but not more.

The practice arose out of the habit of the Government to move the Adjournment of the House if the business of the House was complete before the ordinary hour for the termination of public business (before the war at 11 p.m.). This gave half an hour's "Adjournment" debate before the hour for the automatic Adjournment of the House at eleven-thirty. The half-hour was not available if either the House was discussing "exempted business," or because the House had suspended the eleven o'clock rule, and the proceedings were still continuing at eleven-thirty.

During the war the House sat very much earlier in the day, and normally the hour of rising was at 5.30 instead of 11.30 p.m. The result was that, after the danger of enemy air raids diminished it was often quite feasible to hold half an hour's debate after the termination of the day's business, notwithstanding that the House had risen after the usual hour.

At present the half-hour debate is granted irrespective of the hour at which the day's business is completed, and if the rising is early, the debate lasts for the whole interval (which is sometimes of several hours' duration) between the termination of business and the normal hour appointed for the rising of the House.

The opinion of the House is expressed by resolutions which do not differ greatly in form or substance from such as are common in all debating or deliberating assemblies of whatever sort. Such resolutions have no legal effect, but politically some are of equal importance to the passage of a Bill. Treaties, for instance, are concluded by prerogative of the Crown and require no Act of Parliament to confirm them. Nevertheless, it is customary for a resolution to be proposed in both Houses agreeing with the proposed treaty, and such a treaty is often not considered politically binding until such ratification has taken place. Recently the agreements in connection with the American Loan were subjected to this procedure, and it is probable that any major Act of State not requiring legislation is better confirmed by resolution in this way.

Resolutions are not confined to matters of this kind. Expressions of opinion on any subject may be recorded in this way. In the eighteenth century the famous resolution was proposed that "the power of the Crown has increased, is increasing, and ought to be diminished." Nowadays one of the commonest resolutions to be debated, other than resolutions proposed by the Government, is a resolution of censure. By custom the Government always gives time for the consideration of a motion of censure tabled by any substantial section of the House, and more particularly by the official Opposition.

Even though time for discussion is refused by the Government, Members may put resolutions down for discussion on the Order Paper, and, if they obtain a large number of Members' signatures supporting them, may get for their views a considerable measure of publicity and even affect Government policy. The Member who puts down a resolution, however, is often embarrassed by members of the public who are not yet fully aware of the Government's complete control of time, and write to ask him why he does not bring in his motion for discussion.

CHAPTER XIX

Control of the Executive

THE basic political theory of the Constitution is that Parliament controls the Executive, that is, the Cabinet. An adverse vote in the House of Commons entails the resignation of the Cabinet unless it is soothed by a subsequent vote of confidence or unless the matter is trivial and the Cabinet feels strong enough to continue. No Cabinet can continue in office for an instant if the House of Commons for any reason has lost confidence in it.

The cynic will object that so far from the House of Commons controlling the Cabinet, nowadays the rôles are reversed, and the Cabinet controls the House of Commons. The reader of this book will be able by this time to appreciate just how far this statement is true, and how far it is misleading.

For a number of very good reasons if it were really true that the Cabinet controlled and dominated Parliament it would be no longer true that Britain was a free country. The Constitutional privileges which our ancestors won during their struggle with the Crown have still a vital function in the working of our Cabinet system of Government.

In the first place the House of Commons is the instrument by which the electorate controls the Government, the vital link, that is, in the chain of popular control which makes this country a democracy. The people elect the House of Commons composed of men who have declared their political allegiance to a team of party leaders. But it follows from this that where the people show unmistakably that the form of policy which the party leaders are pursuing is not agreeable to them, Members of the House of Commons know that they disregard such symptoms at their peril.

Two very striking instances in recent years can be given of the real control which an active House of Commons can exercise over the Executive.

(i) The withdrawal of the Hoare-Laval Pact in 1935. The National Government of 1935 had been elected to support the policy of sanctions against Italy in Abyssinia. Members of Parliament were therefore horrified when three weeks later a pact (the Hoare-Laval Pact) was announced quite inconsistent with the terms of this policy. There was an immediate and decisive reaction on the part of Government supporters, and the Pact died almost as soon as it was born.

(ii) Another, and perhaps less dramatic example which occurred in 1934. Just before one of the recesses a new set of Unemployment Regulations had been tabled; during their visits to their constituencies Conservative Members supporting the Government discovered from their constituents that the new regulations were unworkable. The reaction again was such that the regulations were withdrawn.

It is quite clear, therefore, that where public opinion is so sharp as to create a revolt among Government supporters in the House, or where for some other reasons such a revolt occurs, the control of the Executive by the House of Commons is still a reality. What is no longer true is that arguments propounded by an Opposition in the House of Commons have much immediate effect in controlling the Executive. These are designed to have their repercussions outside the House, or of persuading Government supporters to assist them.

This statement of principle can be illustrated by each of the major swings in the political pendulum in the nineteenth century. Peel's defeat in 1846 ushered in a period of Liberal ascendancy. This defeat was primarily a defeat in the House of Commons, and was due to a revolt by his supporters instigated by Disraeli against his abandonment of the principle of protection to which his party had stood committed in the previous election. Peel's action was popular in the country, and if he had carried the party with him Conservatism might easily have been the dominant force in the 'fifties and 'sixties.

The last years of the nineteenth century were years of Conservative predominance. This was due to the Liberal split against Gladstone on the subject of Home Rule. The Conservative defeat in 1906 was primarily due to a revolt against Balfour by Conservative Free Traders, although this did not suffice to defeat Balfour in the House.

There is a more fundamental respect in which the ultimate control of the Executive by the House is of importance. This control is our final guarantee against unconstitutional Government. A Government defeated at the polls does not remain in office. In old days it waited to be beaten in the House. Nowadays, it usually resigns at once. In each case the reason is the same.

Whatever may be the truth of the allegation that Governments control their own supporters too strongly by means of the control of time and the threat of dissolution, a Government cannot remain in office for an instant if it is of another political persuasion to a newly elected House of Commons.

That this is so is due to the legal safeguards invented by our forefathers during the struggle with the Crown in the seventeenth century. These in the main consist in the control of the purse, and the control of the sword.

During the period of the struggle with the Crown, Parliament elaborated a complex and efficient procedure for the control of finance by the House of Commons. This extends both to the expenditure and to the raising of money, and controls not merely the totals spent and raised but the appropriation of particular sums within the totals to particular items of expenditure. The mechanism by which the financial procedure operates consists of three parts—the Committees of the whole House, which examine estimates, and originate money Bills, the main financial legislation for the year consisting of three Parts—the Finance Bill, the Consolidated Fund Bill, and the Appropriation Bill, and the Committee of Public Accounts which scrutinizes the accounts submitted by the Comptroller and Auditor-General.

No Bill the effect of which is the raising or expenditure of money can originate except in pursuance of a resolution passed by a Committee of the whole House.

As soon as the debate on the address in answer to the Speech from the Throne has come to an end, the House of Commons sets up two Committees of the whole House, known respectively as the Committee of Supply and the Committee of Ways and Means.

The function of the Committee of Supply is to authorize the issue of money for the use of the Crown in accordance with the estimates prepared and submitted by the Crown.

The main function of the Committee of Ways and Means is the authorization of the particular taxes whereby the sums authorized by the Committee of Supply—or by some other provision can be raised. The Chancellor of the Exchequer, therefore, introduces his Budget every year in the Committee of Ways and Means.

In addition to the work of these two Committees, most legislation nowadays involves a charge on public funds, and most Bills, therefore, in order to be effective, require a preliminary "money resolution" passed by the whole House to authorize the expenditure or create the charge on public funds. Where the creation of the charge is subsidiary to the main purpose of the Bill these resolutions are ordinarily introduced after the Second Reading of the Bill and before the money clauses are reached in Committee.

When the Committees of Supply and of Ways and Means have passed their resolutions these are reported to the House like other Committee reports and are then considered "in the Report Stage" by the House. Later they are embodied in the three Bills which become the Finance, the Consolidated Fund, and the Appropriation Acts of the Year.

The essential feature of this procedure whereby the control of Parliament is assured lies not in the formal structure of Committees, Acts of Parliament and resolutions, but in the fact that it is not ordinarily the custom of Parliament to grant monies for a period in advance of the current or the ensuing year. The Civil List (as the private revenues of the Crown are called), the Speaker's and judges' salaries and certain other items are excluded from the itemized annual estimates submitted to the Committee of Supply. Certain revenues (like those deriving from Crown Lands) accrue to the Consolidated Fund year by year without inclusion in the annual Finance Bill.

But the main expenditure of the Crown is authorized to be made out of the Consolidated Fund, and the main taxes (including income tax) are legally raised only for periods of twelve months in all. The Government are thus compelled to come to Parliament every year, and in practice much more often to secure the legal right to secure the financial means to carry on their Government.

A second important feature of the system is rule of debate which permits the merit of any grievance connected with the department whose estimates are under consideration, or any of whose expenditure is contributed to by the expenditure contemplated being discussed in detail before the relative financial provision is passed. A narrower ruling might easily have been made. It might easily have been argued that what is under discussion was merely the desirability of raising or expending certain sums of money, and not the efficiency of the department concerned. Fortunately, a more generous construction is allowed.

The result is that a Government cannot avoid criticism of its administrative policy. Every year it has to go to Parliament for more money. Every year the Opposition can discuss the broadest issues before the grant is made, and the private Member the particular complaints of his least important constituents. The widest issues and narrowest issues of policy can be discussed in the estimates, the dismissal of Able Seaman Bloggins, the need for more houses, the broad issues of peace and war, or the complaint of the individual member of the public at the inefficiency of some aspect of the public service—everything, in fact, can be discussed in full which does not require legislation to be remedied, that is, anything for which the Government, as distinct from Parliament itself, must bear the responsibility. The debates on the estimates are, with the King's Speech and motions for the Adjournment of the House, the main engines by which detailed criticism can be deployed against the Government of the day.

The business of seeing that the financial orders of the House are, in fact, obeyed, now rests with the Comptroller and Auditor-General, a public official enjoying absolutely independent status, and the House of Commons Committee of Public Accounts, a Select Committee of fifteen Members appointed yearly, whose meetings are attended by the Comptroller and Auditor-General, who examine his reports. So much for the Control of the Purse. The Sword is equally subject to the House of Commons.

Dating from the same period, that of struggle between the Executive and Parliament, and bearing the same general marks is the Annual Army Act, which provides for the discipline and organization of the Army, now accompanied by the annual Air Force Act, which does the same service for the Air Force. The Navy, which dates from the more tyrannical Tudor times, is a permanent institution whose discipline is controlled by the Naval Discipline Act—a permanent statistic requiring no renewal.[1] The experience of Cromwell's "Major-Generals" and the observation of contemporary Continental monarchies led the Parliaments of Charles the Second's day to license the Army, like the taxes of the realm, only year by year. The object of this was to prevent the Army becoming in Britain as elsewhere the engine of tyranny. A similar procedure was followed during the late war in regard to the Emergency Powers Act, which gave the Government dictatorial power—and it would be agreeable to be able to record that a convention of the Constitution exists whereby any dictatorial or unusual powers

---

[1] It used to be said truly that this was because a navy could not be made the instrument of tyranny. In those days complete naval blockade was not considered a possible weapon of war.

which are found necessary from time to time should be granted by Parliament only for one year. Unhappily when the present Government continued certain of the Emergency Powers after the war they decided to take the powers for a period of five years instead of one year, the Home Secretary expressly admitting that he did so in order to prevent unnecessary criticism on matters of detail. That in doing so he was acting contrary to the spirit of the Constitution will, it is conceived, hardly be denied by constitutional historians or lawyers. However, it must now be sadly admitted that to some extent the control of the Executive under the modern party system rests more as an honourable obligation on the supporters of the Government than upon their open opponents. Even the prolongation of Parliament for strictly party ends by an unscrupulous majority could nowadays only be prevented by the bold use of their powers by the House of Lords.

CHAPTER XX

To-day and To-morrow

NO institution is immortal, and none, if it remains static, can survive. Parliament has survived in the past precisely because under an identity of form it has preserved a continuously, and radically, changing content. Mediæval polity, Tudor despotism, Stuart conflict, Hanoverian aristocracy, bourgeois plutocracy, universal suffrage, all have existed within Parliamentary forms.

Where do we go from here? Has Parliament reached its ultimate development? Will it break down? Can it survive? If so, what changes must it make?

It needs no profound political insight to see that Parliament is labouring under a strain. What is the nature of the strain? Will Parliament stand it? What changes in structure must it undergo?

The first and clear strain is caused by the volume of work, which has increased, is increasing, and shows signs of increasing still further. Look first at the number of Government Departments which exist.

The monarchs of England governed England with a Lord Chancellor, a Lord High Admiral, a Chancellor of the Exchequer, a Lord Treasurer, a pocketful of judges, and later a single Secretary of State.

The Secretaries of State divided into twins, and various Boards began to proliferate. The Lord High Admiral developed into a Board of Admiralty presided over by a First Lord. The Army developed a Secretary for War, and at one time a Secretary at War at the same time. It has now an Army Council under a Secretary of State. The youngest of the three services developed an Air Council on the Army model, and later divided in two and produced a Ministry of Civil Aviation. The Councils of Trade and Plantations developed into the Board of Trade, a fertile mother from which sprang numerous children, the Minister of Fuel and Power, the Ministry of Transport, the Department of Overseas Trade, possibly the Colonial Office (from which came the Dominions Office), and perhaps the Ministries of Production and Supply. Various other Ministries have developed from Boards or Commissions—the Ministry of Education from the Board of

150

Education, the Ministry of Health from the Local Government Board, and the Ministry of Town and Country Planning from the Ministry of Health, the Ministry of Works from the Commissioners of Works, the Ministry of Agriculture from the Board of Agriculture. There is a Scottish Office, an India Office, a Burma Office. A Foreign Office Department developed in war into a Ministry of Information and of the spate of wartime Ministries there is no certain end.

The volume of legislation has developed a hundredfold. The immensely prolix statutes of the eighteenth century gave rise to concentrated and businesslike legislation in the nineteenth. A Liberal Government in 1906-1913 was passing between two and four hundred pages of legislation a year. But from that moment both the number and length of statutes rapidly increased. Conservative and National Governments between the wars passed anything between one and two thousand pages of legislation in a good year and in addition anything up to a thousand pages of Statutory Rules and Orders under powers which it had delegated.

War brought new complexities in administration. Shortages of food, materials and labour, and difficulties of distribution introduced a whole host of sanctions, a whole complexity of administrative machinery, all under the general authority of Parliament and all impinging on the everyday life of the individual at every stage in his existence.

Presumably some of these interferences will end with shortage, but an immense new burden is at this moment to be thrown on a Parliamentary machine already overloaded. The major industries of the country are to be nationalized, and although this does not mean that Parliament will be concerned with day to day problems of administration, for these industries, despite what some of the critics say, are not going to be turned into Government Departments; on Parliament will devolve the same sort of scrutiny and control as ought to be (but seldom is) exercised by a shareholders' meeting.

This immense burden can never be shouldered by Parliament without substantial, perhaps radical alterations in its structure which it is quite impossible to foresee. The question which we have to consider is—can these alterations be made without destroying the essential virtue and character of the Parliamentary system?

There is not likely to be one, simple, Copernican solution of the

F   151

problem. Nor is the solution when found likely to be wholly satisfactory. Life's problems are not solved in this way. Rather the solution will consist in a number of devices, some radical, some small, each concerned with the intention of fully satisfying two divergent principles:

(*a*) To reduce the burden on Parliamentary time.

(*b*) To retain the essence of the matter—that is Government by discussion.

Let us first consider some of the means which might be attempted.

(1) *Delegation to the Cabinet.* The advantage of this solution is that it is simple, efficient, and well tried. It has some distinguished adherents.

The disadvantages are also well known. The first and main point is that it has already been exploited almost up to—some would say beyond—the point of what is consistent with free Government by discussion. Government by regulation, as we have seen, necessarily excludes discussion in Parliament. If it did not there would be no point in it, since its whole object is to reduce the pressure on Parliamentary time.

(2) *Delegation to Local Authorities.* The pressure on Parliamentary time is one of the factors that has led to the recrudescence of respectable bodies of opinion demanding Welsh and Scottish Home Rule. Such enthusiasts do not always observe that their problems are no less acute in England, India and the Colonies, and that other parts of the world for which we are responsible receive even less attention. Nobody gets his affairs discussed adequately in Parliament, because there is not time to discuss them. Yet at the same time great measures of delegation have taken place in local authorities which are already becoming almost as burdened with work as Parliament itself. The whole of our system of national education, most of housing, town planning and public health, and almost all police, fire, water and other services are completely, perhaps excessively decentralized, and further decentralization on a large scale is wholly impossible without either the creation of new local authorities or the reorganization of those which exist.

On the other hand, the supply of men and women of sufficient calibre and public spirit to undertake public work is not unlimited. Indeed, we are already severely strained to man all our local and public authorities, and all our voluntary bodies of organized opinion. It does not look as if there is much hope here. There is some, but not much reason to believe that local Parliaments for England, Scotland, and Wales on the Northern Irish model, would ease the burden, but all this involves extra man-power which would drain Parliament and existing local authorities of their strength, and the public and international disadvantages which would accrue might turn out to be considerable.

. (3) *Delegation to Parliamentary Committees.* Why not split subjects up? Have a Foreign Affairs Committee, a Colonial Problems Committee, Finance, Trade and Industries, Education, Agricultural Committees? And treat Parliament much as local authorities are treated—bodies for the reception or reference back of reports from Committees?

This scheme has many adherents. To some extent it is already adopted by the American Congress, and informally both the Parties in Parliament have adopted it for the purpose of their internal arrangements.

It involves, however, two separate difficulties. In the first place it ignores the fact that in sovereign bodies, as distinct from local authorities, policy must be regarded as a coherent whole. Guns or butter is a real choice, but it is far more complicated than that. What proportion of your national assets and energy are you prepared to spend on guns, butter, education, houses, old people, young people, middle-aged people, capital, consumption, food, police, and so on? This problem, which is the fundamental problem of government, cannot be discussed in separate Committees, cannot be discussed divorced from detail, and yet must be discussed in general principle. General discussion in the House of Commons is the only way.

The second difficulty is that the solution strikes at the root of our present system of Government. You can either govern through an Executive responsible to Parliament supported by a majority party as at present, or you can govern by a system of all-party Committees as do County Councils. So far no means have been discovered of marrying the two systems. Perhaps the future may prove more fortunate.

(4) *Revolutionize Parliamentary Procedure.* This solution is being tried by the Government at the time, and a Select Committee, with a plentiful supply of enthusiastic new Members is discussing the question "upstairs," and has already issued an interim report. Committees of the whole House on Bills are to be

restricted, Standing Committees multiplied, and a time-table imposed on their proceedings.

There is something, but not much, which can be done on these lines. What takes the time is not the forms of procedure which are almost infinitely flexible, but the need to express and discuss the different points of view, not only between parties, but between Members of all parties.

(5) Nor can it successfully be maintained that it is possible greatly to increase the hours or times of sitting. We shall see the opinions of Mr. Churchill on this point [1] vigorously, perhaps even a little too strongly expressed.

(6) I sometimes toy with the idea that you can delegate up instead of down. If we had a World Parliament to discuss international problems would we not have more time to discuss our own affairs? But quite obviously a World Parliament, which I will consider later, would never be introduced for the purpose of reforming Parliamentary procedure— except in looking-glass land, where it would no doubt happen this way.

A by-product of the changes in our social structure and of the pressure on Parliamentary time is the difficulty of finding suitable candidates. A man must live and cannot live without loaves and fishes. I venture to say (with due humility to my unmarried friends) that a public man *must* be happily married and *should* have a family. To make life worth living for these companions in life's journey is a first charge on the time of any one who undertakes these responsibilities. In old days a public man had ample leisure, and in any event usually came from a class with ample means as often as not "derived from land"—but in any event derived from investments. When I look at Victorian prints of the House of Commons, a collection of top-hatted, bewhiskered and infinitely dignified gentlemen, I often think:

"They toil not neither do they spin, yet even Solomon in all his glory was not arrayed like one of these."

I often wonder what a Victorian M.P. would think of me as I clean out the kitchen boiler of a morning, or cook the breakfast, or wash up the dishes.

A man must have the constitution of an ox apart from all the other necessary qualities to stand up to the life of a Member of Parliament nowadays.

[1] See p. 172.

A recent author [1] has demonstrated that at present it is virtually impossible for anyone without means to be a Member of Parliament unless he belongs to one of two or three chosen professions—Trade Union officialdom, Journalism, the Bar—or is a Company Director. Is this satisfactory?

What is the solution? I say—pay them more. I know the objections, and I still say pay them more.

I venture to quote, for the first time, with some changes, from a memorandum I submitted to the Select Committee at present considering remuneration for Members' of Parliament.

MEMORANDUM FOR THE SELECT COMMITTEE OF MEMBERS SALARIES AND EXPENSES

(1) I have been a Member of Parliament since 1938. During this time I have never failed to satisfy the Income Tax Inspectors that my expenses as a Member of Parliament exclusive of Election expenses and of charitable donations amounted to something more than £600 a year. From April 13th, 1945, until the fall of the Caretaker Government, I was Under-Secretary of State for Air with a salary of £1,500. During this period none of my expenses as a Member of Parliament which remained constant were deductible from my salary as Minister. In the result, regarding salary and emoluments only, it was a net gain to me of about £150 a year to have been appointed Minister, but in fact I lost a considerable sum net, since I was debarred from earning money as a journalist and an author during that time.

(2) During the period for which I have been a Member of Parliament the cost of living has risen by a sum which so far as Members of Parliament are concerned is certainly in excess of the official cost of living figure. For instance, when I became a Member I was able to employ a secretary at not more than £2 10s. per week. The salary now for a good secretary is £5 5s. a week. Other expenses have not all risen in proportion, but they have risen by a figure which I do not estimate at less than 50 per cent.

(3) I have made some enquiries as to the salaries of Members of Parliament outside this country—in the British Dominions and in America. It is well known that Congressmen receive 10,000 dollars a year with allowances for offices and two secretaries. I understand it is proposed to increase this salary by something like 50 per cent. The position of a Congressman is not completely

[1] Mr. J. F. S. Ross in "Parliamentary Representation."

analogous to that of a British Member of Parliament since he has a larger number of constituents and Washington is further from his constituency as compared with any British constituency. His expenses are therefore greater and his inability to earn his living as a result of his Membership to Congress may be more complete. I do not therefore regard the high salary payable to Congressmen as a precedent for putting up the salary of British Members of Parliament or Junior Ministers by a comparable sum. On the other hand, it is a good precedent for paying them reasonably. So far as I can make out the British House of Commons is the worst paid in all the Dominions, including, I understand, the provincial legislatures of Canada.

(4) So far as the average expenses of Members of Parliament are concerned, I should direct the attention of the Committee to a recent book, "Parliamentary Representation," by Mr. J. F. S. Ross, at Chapter XV. So far as I understand the matter, the facts are generally correctly stated in this book. The only criticism I offer is that he has estimated the cost of a conscientious membership of the House of Commons at rather too low a figure for an active Member. His conclusion was:

"It may therefore be estimated that, in normal circumstances, a man needs a private income of from, say, £900 to £2,000 a year to be a Liberal Member of Parliament.

"A man cannot normally be a Conservative Member of Parliament unless he possesses a private income of from £1,500 to £5,000 a year.

"An Independent Member can hardly hope to pay his way without a private income of at least £1,200 a year.

"A working-class Member (of the Labour Party) may need roughly £350 a year in addition to his salary of £600."

All these figures are presumably at 1938 prices.

I do not think the differences between the parties are as great as the author represents, and if they are, I feel certain that the differences will tend to level themselves out to a great extent since the figure required by a Labour Member will tend to become greater and the figure possessed by a Conservative will tend to become less. What does emerge from this extraordinary position is that anybody who does not belong to one or two or three chosen professions (Journalism, the Law or Trade Union Officialdom) cannot hope to be a Member of Parliament and bring up a family unless he has substantial private means.

(5) In my opinion the situation revealed by the above facts is wholly unsatisfactory. The work done by Members of Parliament has multiplied three or four times since the beginning of the century owing to the vast increase of constituency work brought about by the development of the modern administrative state, and owing to the greatly increased length of the sittings. Whereas in 1900 a membership of Parliament could be carried on efficiently as at best a half-time job, in modern times conscientious Members of Parliament must put in at least as much work as the ordinary member of a profession not in the busiest practice. In addition to this he must somehow possess or earn an income of (I estimate) anything up to £1,000 a year.

I should draw the attention of the Committee to the judgment of Lord Snell quoted in "Our Parliament," by S. Gordon (Hansard Society, 1945) as follows:—

> "As a result of seven years' experience, I am convinced that the average Member of Parliament works at greater pressure and for longer hours than nine-tenths of those who elected him, and that if the factory worker, miner or engineer had the same strain put upon him he would down tools within a month and demand better conditions of work."

(6) It is said against a substantial increase of salary that thereby a professional class of politician will arise.

The fact is, of course, that one has already arisen and has existed for some time. The great majority of Members of Parliament have perforce to treat their interest in politics as a part-time employment, but it would be difficult to see what other occupation Pitt, Disraeli, or Mr. Gladstone had during their lives or Mr. Churchill at the present time. In the case of Disraeli the greater part of his life was in opposition and unpaid. In old days it was possible for such men to draw their livelihood from substantial personal wealth, but this is not now the case, and it is a pure matter of accident that a man in Mr. Churchill's position happens also to be a writer and lecturer of genius. As a matter of fact, many Members of Parliament are indirectly subsidized in respect of their political activities, but they draw their emoluments from sources other than the State.

Members in the Labour Party, frequently, perhaps usually, receive emoluments from organizations affiliated to their party which they happen to serve, sometimes directly increased by reason of their representing them in Parliament. But this is not confined to Party or to the back benches. Ministers in recent governments after their resignation have clearly begun to receive salaries from various sources, which it is doubtful if they would have been offered in all cases were they not statesmen of high standing. If they had not received these salaries they could not have continued their public work.

The number of Members who after a period of membership of Parliament can return on competitive terms to a profession or trade and still carry on their membership of Parliament is extremely limited.

(7) Before making my recommendations on this matter, I feel I should point out that my own interest is less than the average of a Member of Parliament. I am the heir to a peerage and cannot hope to benefit for a very long period from any improvements in the status of Members of the House of Commons. Moreover, I have been in some respects fortunate in that I have never found it difficult to earn money in journalism or from the exercise of my profession at the Bar. These advantageous facts enable me to take a somewhat more detached point of view than some others who are less fortunately placed than myself. I therefore recommend:

(1) That the salaries of Junior Ministers should be made up to not less than £2,500 a year, and their expenses as Members of Parliament be deductable from it for the purpose of income tax. This might be done either by permitting a small increased salary to be drawn in addition to the salary of a Member of Parliament or by increasing the salary of the Minister by a greater amount.

(2) I consider that the salaries of Members of Parliament should not be less than £1,500 a year. I arrive at this figure by the following considerations. Allowing for the increase in expenses the figure of £900 per annum would simply put the position where it was in 1938, and I consider that this position was unsatisfactory. I consider that a further £600 per annum at least is necessary for a Member of Parliament to live at all respectably and do his work conscientiously with the secretarial assistance he requires. I do not consider that he should be debarred from earning additional sums by part-time work in other spheres. It is impossible to assess in terms of money at all, the value of the public functions

of a Member of Parliament, but the work which a good
Member of Parliament does for individuals in his constituency would amount in the open market in my judgment
to not less than £2,000 a year. I do not consider that a
Member of Parliament should be paid at the market rate.
The figure of £1,500 in my own case would work out at
£750 expenses and £750 taxable income.

(3) I do not consider that Members of Parliament should be
given any allowances in respect of expenses in addition to
their travelling as at present, as I consider these are either
an inducement to inefficiency or an inducement to dis-
honesty according as to whether an account has to be given
or the money can be drawn in any event. The only solution
is to put the salary of Members of Parliament at a reasonable figure and leave them to pay their own expenses out of
this sum. They will then have an inducement to efficiency
in so far that they will share in any savings they can reasonably make, and an inducement to spend the money which
the work requires in so far that they can claim a refund of
income tax if they do so.

(4) It may be said that these proposals are somewhat revolutionary in their scope. My answer is that the situation
requires a radical solution. The position and functions of a
Member of Parliament have changed radically from the
time when it was assumed that any Member of the House
of Commons would have a sufficiency of income to live
independently of his public functions, and when it was also
assumed that membership of the House of Commons
required comparatively small part of a Member's time. I
should point out that from the early part of the eighteenth
century until about the middle of the nineteenth, a Member
of Parliament had to subscribe a statutory declaration that
he was in possession of an income of not less than
£600 a year derived from land at a time when taxation was
negligible and the value of money very much greater than
it is now.

In these circumstances it is in my judgment completely
and absolutely certain that unless a radical solution is
achieved of this extraordinary complicated and difficult
problem one of two and possibly both of two serious evils
will inevitably arise sooner or later. Either the House of

Commons will be deprived of an adequate supply of men of sufficient quality to undertake its duties or the standard of morality which is now of the highest, and which has been built up by centuries of struggle, will diminish, as I already detect some signs that it is beginning to do.

CHAPTER XXI

The Curtailment of Discussion

FOR a year of Parliamentary work the Government has a session of approximately 200 Parliamentary days of which Mondays to Thursdays are worth seven hours and a half each, and Fridays about an hour less. The first hour of every day, except Fridays, is taken up with questions—and probably an average of another five minutes a day for statements, private notice questions, business questions, personal explanations and the like.

Of the time which remains, twenty days before August 5th are earmarked as days for the estimates, and in addition the Government will require to allow at least a Parliamentary week for the Debate on the Address, and make provision for the Budget, the Finance Bill, the Consolidated Fund, and Appropriation Bills, the Army and Air Force (Annual) Bills,[1] and any Supplementary Estimates before they consider their programme of legislation.

In addition to this they will be extremely lucky to get off with less than two debates on Foreign Affairs (apart from that on the estimates Foreign Office vote), and may perhaps have to face one or more votes of censure. The last half hour of every day's work is useless for contentious Government business, being earmarked for unopposed business or the Adjournment debate and the last day of every sittings is also given up to the Adjournment.

Before the war, the Government's problem was further complicated by the fact that Wednesdays and Fridays before Easter (and certain Fridays after Easter) were given over respectively to private Members' motions, and private Members' Bills, none of which, unless given a supplementary ration of Government time, ever normally saw the Statute Book. Private Members' time was abolished during the war—owing to the abolition of Monday sittings, and the institution of shorter hours owing to the blackout—and has not been restored by the present Government on the resumption of more normal sittings. It may be doubted whether private Members' time will ever occur again.

By this it should be clear to the reader that the main problem

[1] See p. 148.

before a modern Parliament or a modern Government is the pressure on Parliamentary time, and the closer one studies modern Parliamentary forms and procedure the more clearly does the effect of this pressure appear to have left its mark on our manner of doing business.

This appears in two ways: (i) the gradual monopoly of all Parliamentary time by Government business, and (ii) the gradual curtailment both of the theoretical right of discussion and the actual exercise of the right by a private Member. This struggle for time by the Executive has been going on with ever increasing intensity for close on two hundred years and has had a marked effect on our political life.

The original rule of the House was that all Members were equal, and this rule continued long after the Cabinet had become the recognized organ of Government. It is still the basis of the personal relationship between Ministers and Members of Parliament.

In accordance with this principle, at first business put down by one Member had no precedence over business put down by any other. By 1800, however, the Government had found it necessary to reserve one day in every week for business selected by the Government. By 1837 the number of days was already two, and in 1852 this number was increased to three. By 1939 the only free days were the Wednesdays and Fridays before Easter, and, as has been seen, of these only the Fridays were free for private Members' Bills. Except in the rarest instances, and then only with Government support, the right of private Members to initiate legislation had been completely abolished. Even the nominal right is now suspended and perhaps has disappeared for ever.

The same tendency is seen in the duration of debates upon which depends, of course, the effective right of individual Members to be heard. As the original rule was that any Member could initiate business, so it also was that any Member could speak on business, and debates could therefore go on almost indefinitely. When Disraeli spoke as a private Member to introduce a motion advocating the amalgamation of the Consular and diplomatic services in 1842 (a reform not actually carried out until almost exactly one hundred years later), he made a speech of two and a half hours. The Budget debate in 1852 began on December 3rd with a five-hour speech by the Chancellor. The division was taken at 4 a.m. on Friday, December 17th. In a famous Foreign Affairs debate, Palmerston defended his conduct on the "Don Pacifico" incident in a five-hour speech which lasted from before sunset on one summer's night until after dawn the next morning. It was when riding on the morning after this debate that Peel fell from his horse on Constitution Hill and received fatal injuries.

Nowadays, such deliberation would be treated as intolerable long-windedness. The Speaker begins to show signs of impatience when a private Member speaks as long as half an hour, and although a Budget speech is allowed rather more than a full two hours, the usual time for Government or Front Bench Opposition speeches is between forty-five minutes and an hour and a quarter. The longest debate (apart from that on the address) is normally one or two days; a three-day debate is not by any means a common event even on a vote of censure.

The third respect, and the most important, in which discussion has been curtailed is in the mutilation of the rules of procedure. This dates in the main from Mr. Gladstone's period of struggle with the Irish obstructionists in the Parliament which began in 1880.

Until this time the rules of procedure gave the private Member very considerable scope. Members could move the Adjournment of the House before the Orders of the Day or at any time to draw attention to topics which interested them, and this and other rules, including the almost unlimited right of speech, rendered it possible for a minority of Members to block the whole passage of business by the use of the rules for the purpose. The fact that this possibility was not exploited until 1880 and has to this day never been exploited in the House of Lords, where the procedure is unreformed, says much for British Parliamentarians.

From 1880 onwards, the Irish Nationalists ceased to regard their campaign for the self-government of Ireland in terms of Parliamentary opposition, but thought of it more and more in terms of violence and civil war.

The first and most moderate way in which this violence appeared, was by deliberate obstruction. Within a matter of days the Irishmen had reduced the business of the House of Commons almost to a standstill, and its Members to a state bordering on physical exhaustion.

The result was that Gladstone felt himself compelled to introduce radical alterations in the procedure of Parliament which have dominated Parliamentary procedure ever since. It is for this reason that in classifying the history of Parliament into certain periods I made my fifth and last period, that of the modern Parliament, date from the Gladstonian reforms in 1880 and the following years.

The most important of these reforms were:—

(1) The Closure. This is a motion which a Member may move in the middle of a discussion on any subject which appears to that Member to have been going on long enough. It is normally moved by a supporter of the Government or even a Minister who desires to curtail the length to which the Opposition are protracting the debate. The motion is proposed by the Member rising in his place and saying: "Mr. Speaker, I beg to move that the question be now put." If the Speaker considers this to be an abuse of the rights of free speech he may refuse to accept it—but otherwise the motion must be put to the House without any debate. If it is carried, and if it is proposed by a Government supporter, of course it always is carried, the effect is to bring the debate to a close before the discussion has reached a natural conclusion. How oppressive this may prove to a minority need hardly be stressed; their only protection is the Speaker, and the rule is so framed that he cannot intervene, unless he considers the motion an abuse of the rules.

(2) The "eleven o'clock rule."[1] This rule brings the debate to a close automatically at a specified hour (nowadays 9.15 p.m.) unless the subject under discussion is "exempted business" or unless the rule has been specifically suspended.

(3) The "Kangaroo" Closure. This was the most beneficial and the least oppressive of all Mr. Gladstone's reforms. It gives to the Chair power in Committee or elsewhere to pass over amendments which it considers unimportant or unnecessary to secure a fair discussion of all points. This results in a considerable saving of time, and though perhaps it is not a particularly logical way of doing things, it has worked well.

(4) The "Guillotine" Closure. This procedure is the most drastic of all and the hardest to justify. It is an arrangement by which the Government compels the House by the use of its majority to accept a time-table for the passage of a particular piece of legislation. If the business is not transacted by the time allotted, divisions on all outstanding motions must take place without further discussion. This procedure was first used in 1887,

[1] See p. 174.

and has been employed by most administrations since that date. But it is deservedly unpopular and is always bitterly resented by the official Opposition of whatever party.

(5) The right to move the Adjournment on the initiative of a private Member was limited to cases where leave is given under a procedure discussed elsewhere [1] to move it in order to discuss a "definite matter of urgent public importance." It is almost easier for a camel to pass through the eye of a needle than for a Member of Parliament to secure a debate by means of this procedure.

That Mr. Gladstone's reforms mutilated Parliamentary procedure can hardly be open to doubt. His justification must be that what he did has been embraced and accepted by Governments of all political complexions since his time, even though organized obstruction, which can never succeed where it is not supported by popular opinion in the constituencies of the Members obstructing, is at present, at least, a thing of the past.

The fact is that the Irish were an occasion only. The pressure of modern business is such that Parliament can maintain control only at the price of self-abnegation in the matter of discussion, and the Government can get through its programme only at the price of some sort of coercion of the minority. But this does not diminish the inherent danger in what is being done. We are very near the bone now and any considerable further development of the tendencies would convert Parliament from a free assembly into a Reichstag. The borderline is a narrow one, and could easily be stepped over.

In two important respects Governments have already gone beyond what was done by Mr. Gladstone.

The first of these is the extended use of delegated legislation. As the father of the first series of changes was Mr. Gladstone, so the father of the modern use of this device was Mr. Asquith. By 1911 it had been found impossible even with the truncated procedure to get through the legislative programme of the session. Moreover, the machinery which had to be set up to administer the new Social Insurance Legislation typified by the National Health Insurance Act required a series of regulations far too complex and requiring modification far too frequently to be embodied as a Schedule or series of Schedules to the Act. Ministerial regulations and Orders in Council were therefore resorted to—a device which had always been employed to enact regulations

[1] See p. 141.

either in those cases where the Crown was empowered to do so under the Prerogative, or where Acts of Parliament gave the Crown power to do so.

Since 1911 most Acts of Parliament have conferred wide powers on the Minister most chiefly concerned to enact, either by regulation or through the Crown by Orders in Council, the widest possible powers to make rules and orders with the force of law for the purpose of carrying out the policy of the Act. During both World Wars a general power of legislation by regulation for the purposes of the war has been conferred, under which almost all the liberties of the subject were curtailed or abolished.

During the years before the war the Statutory Rules and Orders enacted by Conservative or National Ministers averaged something like one thousand pages of closely printed type per year—and in the main each annual volume was in addition to and not in substitution for the regulations of the year before. The present Labour Government has secured new emergency powers to legislate generally in regard to the distribution and price of goods and services for a period of five years.

The effect of this practice has been largely to restore to the Crown the power of legislation without Parliament which it lost in the seventeenth century.

The difference between regulations contained in a Schedule to a Bill and regulations by "delegated legislation," is that Parliament has no power to amend the latter, whereas the former have to go through the detailed scrutiny of a "Committee Stage" which has already been described.

The only control exercised by Parliament over Statutory Rules and Orders is what is called the right of "prayer." Under this procedure a regulation which a Minister makes in pursuance of a power conferred by an Act has to be laid on the Tables of the Houses of Parliament for a period of, usually, forty days. If during that time a Member puts down, and carries, a resolution that the regulation be annulled, it ceases to have effect. The disadvantages of this procedure are that it leaves the initiative to the scrutiny of an individual Member who happens to dislike a regulation, and that even by prayer amendment is impossible. It frequently happens that the objectionable feature is a relatively small point in a lengthy and complicated series of regulations, and the House is naturally unwilling to annul the whole of these and thereby throw a complex piece of administrative machinery into disorder merely on what would be regarded as a minor "Committee point" if the regulations formed part of a Bill.

To meet these objections a permanent Select Committee was instituted during the Coalition Government on the initiative of Mr. Herbert Morrison. The purpose of this Committee is to perform the function which otherwise would have to be undertaken by private Members, of scrutinizing Orders in Council and reporting to the House if they contain objectionable features or unusual powers. The weakness of this Committee is that it cannot concern itself with the policy of regulations and therefore necessarily confines itself to matters of form rather than the substantial policy pursued by Ministers.

At one time delegated legislation was thought to be subject to the Courts. An Act would say, "if such and such is necessary for the purpose of the Act, the Minister may by regulation prescribe . . .," and where this phraseology was followed a Court of Law was competent to inquire whether or no the regulation was in fact reasonably necessary for the purpose in question.

This was obviously undesirable, since the effect was to make the Courts, which have in their own interest to remain strictly non-political, inquire into the necessity of policy. The modern practice, therefore, is to make the Act provide for regulation: *"Where in the opinion of the Minister it is necessary."* Where this form of words is used the only question which the Court can consider is not whether the regulation is necessary but whether the Minister considered it necessary. This has the effect of almost completely removing the power of a Court to enquire into this regulation.

There is nothing to show that the developments of the past fifty years have ceased to extend their scope. Since the new Parliament has come into being, not merely has the Government extended its power of legislation by decree, but it has set up a Committee on Procedure which has already decided to impose on every Bill sent upstairs to a Standing Committee a sort of permanent "guillotine" or fixed time-table.

No institution is immortal. Its continued existence depends on the extent to which its forms can be made to serve the changed needs of successive generations and periods. In the past Parliament in general, and the House of Commons in particular, has shown the most amazing versatility. Under the forms of a mediæval society which to some extent it still maintains, it has served

167

successively the varied purposes of a feudal monarchy, a Tudor depotism, a political revolution transferring the control from the Crown to a committee of landowners, a nineteenth-century government by the middle class, a modern democracy at war with a dictatorship. This versatility is the more surprising because the House of Commons and Parliament have remained despite their changes, recognizably the same throughout and stand to-day as the identical institution which gathered under the first Edward and served this country throughout its varied history.

But longevity gives no guarantee of continued existence, still less of unabated vigour. The line which divides a Reichstag from a free assembly is not so easily drawn as might be supposed. A free assembly is one which effectively controls the policy of the executive and legislation; a Reichstag, a body existing solely in order to register decisions arrived at elsewhere. Mere freedom of speech is not enough. The control which a modern Executive exercises over the legislature is already such as to make it difficult to see how much further changes can safely proceed.

The extent to which the control of Parliament by Cabinet had proceeded by 1939 was thus summed up by Professor Keith.

"It must be remembered that the Members of the Commons have only limited opportunities of attacking effectively the policy of the Cabinet. The King's Speech at the opening of Parliament affords one opportunity. Twenty to twenty-three days are devoted to supply, when criticism is possible of the matters covered by the votes put down which are usually selected as desired by the Opposition. On four occasions when the House goes into Committee to consider the three sets of defence and the Civil Estimates motions may be brought forward if the ballot favours the mover, as when in 1937 foreign policy was debated in the Civil Estimates. On the motions for the Easter and Whitsunday Adjournment, issues can be raised as they can be each night when the House is about to adjourn, and in cases of urgency approved by the Speaker, a motion for the Adjournment may be accepted and brought on at 7.30 p.m. A motion of censure by the Opposition will certainly receive a due allocation of time, for a Government which shirks facing such a motion would lose standing in a very marked degree. Finally legislative proposals afford a constant opportunity for criticism both in principle and in detail.

But this list of opportunities leaves after all comparatively little scope for Members to raise issues other than those which the Government finds it necessary to submit to the Commons. When the Ministry can act without legislation the opportunities for criticism are reduced and in the operation of prerogative or statutory powers a Ministry has a very free hand. The essential feature of the exercise of these powers is that the Ministry may take decisions and then confront the Commons with a *fait accompli*."

In May, 1844, a political novel by one Benjamin Disraeli caused quite a flutter among the literary and political circles in London. The book contained some fantastic, and many unorthodox comments and epigrams on English political history, many of them put into the mouth of a mysterious oriental magnate called Sidonia.

"You will observe one curious trait," said Sidonia to Coningsby, "in the history of this country. The depository of power is always unpopular. All combine against it. It always falls. Power was deposited in the great Barons. The Church, using the King for its instrument, crushed the great Barons. Power was deposited in the Church. The King, bribing the Parliament, plundered the Church. Power was deposited in the King. The Parliament, using the People, beheaded the King, expelled the King, changed the King, and finally for a King substituted an administrative officer. For one hundred and fifty years Power has been deposited in the Parliament, and for the past sixty or seventy years it has been becoming more and more unpopular. . . . As we see that the Barons, the Church, the King, have in turn devoured each other, and that the Parliament, the last devourer, remains, it is impossible to resist the impression that this body also is doomed to be destroyed, and he is a sagacious statesman who may detect in what form and in what quarter the Great Consumer will arise."

No one would treat this curious set of paradoxes as an exact account of British Constitutional development, and it was apparently Mr. Disraeli's opinion at the time that the great consumer would arise in the form of a revived, a purified Crown and aristocracy—a view which was less mistaken at the time than might be thought, because it was exactly what happened in contemporary Germany to her own irretrievable ruin.

But Disraeli was a better prophet than he knew, or than many of the more orthodox historians. The great consumer has indeed arisen, and has arisen in a sense in the restored prerogatives of the Crown. The great consumer is the Executive, fortified by the Civil Service, whose devoted labours an opposition, however talented, cannot command; reinforced by the control of the time of Parliament, armed with the weapon of dissolution, and in undisputed control of the party machine of the dominant political organism of the House of Commons.

CHAPTER XXII

Times and Seasons

THE life of Parliament is in a sense a continuous tradition stretching back for seven hundred years. No Parliament for many centuries has failed to contain a large number, often a majority of Members who served in the last. None has failed to contain at least a few who have recollections of the service of the House for very many years before. To this fact, to the permanence of its records and officials, and to its fixed seat at Westminster, Parliament owes the great antiquity and continuity of its methods, and its traditional procedure.

Strictly speaking, however, the life of a Parliament is extremely short. A Parliament comes into being as the result of the issue of writs of summons issued from the Crown Office in pursuance of a Royal Proclamation and Order in Council, and comes to an end as the result of the use of the Royal Prerogative of Dissolution. In legal theory a Parliament can also expire by effluxion of time (five years under the Parliament Act, 1911), but this does not happen in practice, since when a Parliament is nearing the legal term of its life the Government always chooses its own selected moment to "go to the country" on a dissolution.

In practice, the only period for which there is no Parliament is the minimum period necessary for a General Election: in strict legal theory Parliament need only meet once in three years. In political fact, Government for even six months would be impossible without Parliament, and after a year taxes would cease to be payable and the Army no longer legally subject to discipline.[1]

The formal life of Parliament is broken up into Sessions. These are in practice approximately a year in length, although there is no fixed legal limit. A Session is brought to an end by the exercise of the Royal prerogative of prorogation, which is effected at the close of a Session by an announcement made in the House of Lords by the King in person or by Commissioners appointed by him for that purpose. The prorogation usually takes place immediately after the Royal Assent has been given to any Bills which remain unassented to after having passed both Houses.

[1] See p. 144 ff.

A Bill which has not received the Royal Assent by the end of the Session dies without becoming law, and has to be reintroduced again from the beginning.

The actual sitting of the House is broken up into periods of sitting and periods of recess. This is done by the simple process of adjournment by resolution of the Houses themselves.

In actual fact, of course, since under the working of the Constitution the Government controls a majority of the House of Commons, the Government arrange the dates of sittings, the date of prorogation, and the date of dissolution, and the formal apparatus of Royal prerogative and proclamation; even the resolution of the Houses themselves is little more than legal machinery.

As a rule the sittings of the House take place during a period of about nine months in the year with a recess of a month at Christmas, shorter recesses at Easter and Whitsun, and a long recess for two months at least during August and September. This is not invariable, and not entirely accurate, but broadly speaking the above picture gives a fair impression. The prorogation often takes place after the House has reassembled after the long summer recess, and after it has transacted some business. Although a more formal break in the life of the Parliament it may not give rise to an actual break in the sittings for more than a day, the Houses reassembling immediately to hear the King's Speech.

Ought Parliament to meet more frequently? When the House goes into recess a Member or two can almost always be heard to complain that it is an indecent thing for the House to suspend its labours at a time when so many urgent problems still clamour for solution.

During the Parliament of 1935-45 this Member was often Mr. Shinwell, now Minister of Fuel and Power. His complaints are not heard now that he is in Office, and the periods of recess are not noticeably very different.

The fact is that Parliament probably meets for the maximum period consonant with its efficient working. In the opinion of one distinguished and experienced Parliamentarian it meets far too long.[1]

"If you wish to say what is wrong with Parliament," observed Mr. Winston Churchill to the Select Committee on Procedure in

---

[1] Quoted from "Our Parliament," by S. Gordon, Hansard Society, 1945, as is the quotation which immediately follows.

1931, "it is that it sits far too long in the year. I would lay down that except in times of war or great national emergency Parliament should not sit more than five months with the ordinary short intervals, say, occupying six months of the year."

And again in Parliament as Prime Minister on November 29th, 1944, Mr. Churchill said:

"Do not suppose that you can strengthen Parliament by wearying it, and in keeping it in almost continuous session. If you want to reduce the power of Parliament, let it sit every day in the year, one-fifth part filled, and then you will find it will be the laughing-stock of the nation, instead of being, as it continues to be, in spite of all the strains of modern life, the citadel as well as the cradle of Parliamentary institutions throughout the world: almost the only successful instance of a legislative body with plenary powers, elected on a universal suffrage, which is capable of discharging with restraint and with resolution, all the functions of peace and war."

The truth is that Parliament and its Members are torn between two equal and opposite strains—the immense volume of work which needs to be done, and the need to keep itself constantly qualified to do it. A Member of Parliament cannot visit his constituency, except somewhat irregularly at week-ends while Parliament sits, and cannot travel or read at all. The work of the Departments cannot proceed at full speed until Parliament has risen. Ministers regard the recesses as the periods during which they can achieve their most valuable work in their Offices. On the other hand, the volume of legislation is such that there is no hope in the near future of getting back to the five monthly sessions visualized by Mr. Churchill.

During the sittings Parliament sits on five days during the week—on Mondays, Tuesdays, Wednesdays and Thursdays in the afternoon and evening, and on Fridays in the morning and afternoon. The Friday "half holiday," which is said to owe its origin to Sir Robert Walpole's predilection for field sports, has a usefulness at the present day in that it permits Members with distant constituencies to spend at least a day in their constituencies during the week-end.

Originally the House used to meet in the mornings: it was found, however, that it was more convenient for the House to meet in the afternoons in order to permit Ministers to attend at their offices during the mornings, and Members to deal with correspondence, Committees or private business. Before the war the sittings, other than Fridays, began at 2.45 p.m., and on Fridays at eleven.

During the war sittings were in the mornings and afternoons owing to the absence of trains and buses late in the evening. After the danger of air raids had diminished during the last few months of the war afternoon sittings were resumed, but they began at 2.15 instead of 2.45. These are the hours at present.[1] The Friday sittings begin at eleven in the morning.

Originally, there was no time at which the sittings had to end, but the period of obstruction by the Irish Party put an end to this as to other easy-going English habits.

Before the war the order was that at 11 p.m. on Mondays, Tuesdays, Wednesdays and Thursdays, the business of the House comes to an end, and that except for proceedings on the closure and the "half-hour Adjournment" only unopposed business might be taken after that hour. Under this rule the House stood adjourned at half-past eleven automatically without question put. This rule still operates, but at present the hour of 9.15 p.m. stands instead of 11 p.m. and 9.45 p.m. instead of 11.30.

The Friday debate is now concluded at 5.30 p.m.

In any event there are certain types of business (known as "exempted business") to which the so-called "eleven o'clock rule" does not apply, and in cases where it is desired to extend the time available for any debate, the Government may propose and carry a resolution at the beginning of the day's business "suspending the rule." This may be done indefinitely or, since 1943, for a specified period of, say, one or two hours. Where the rule is suspended indefinitely or the business is exempted business if there are enough speakers, the House may still enjoy an all-night sitting.

The House may, of course, meet at any time or in any place it thinks fit in case of emergency. The sitting at which the declaration of war was announced, September 3rd, 1939, was on a Sunday morning, and many of the wartime Sessions were in Church House, Westminster.

The House of Lords normally meets at 2.15. There is no "eleven o'clock rule," but late sittings are extremely exceptional.

[1] Since writing the above the hours have been changed and are now 2.30 p.m. to 10.30 p.m.

CHAPTER XXIII

Comparisons and Queries

A DISCUSSION of the future of Parliament leads us inevitably to ask what to me is the ultimate question.

What is the essence of Parliamentary Government? How much of our own is historical accident, how much is its essential nature? How much applies to ourselves alone? How much is of universal application? Assuming, as I most confidently believe, that Government by discussion is a good, indeed the only good, form of Government what are the conditions for its existence and survival?

I have come to the conclusion that these conditions are five in number. Given most of these, Parliamentary Government will be successful.

The conditions are:—

(1) The material condition. Military and economic security.
(2) The practical condition. A strong executive and an organized opposition.
(3) The moral condition. Recognition by the Parliament of the rights of man or the natural law.
(4) The Parliamentary conditions, consisting of four main principles:
    (i) Absolute freedom of speech, subject only to self-imposed rules of order.
    (ii) Autonomy in matters of procedure.
    (iii) The widest possible publicity to proceedings.
    (iv) Patriotism rising above party.
(5) The electoral condition. Universal adult suffrage.

I do not believe that Parliamentary Government can succeed, or survive unless most of these conditions are present in some measure.

Without any fault of the Parliament's own, military weakness or war, or economic confusion can so disorganize life as to make free government impossible. The last fifteen years have, I should imagine, demonstrated this fairly clearly. I come to this conclusion inevitably. Either a Parliament must rule the World of Nations and finance, or else tyranny or disorder will destroy Parliaments.

Secondly, good Parliaments can be destroyed when there is no strong Executive. A Government must govern with the consent of Parliament, but it must govern. Weakness or chaos is the ultimate fate of all assemblies not led by strong Executives. It follows from this that as a counterpoise there must be a vigorous Parliamentary opposition strongly rooted in the constituencies.

Thirdly, I cannot disregard the moral factor. Parliament was made for man, not man for Parliament. No man, no institution, no body of men, no class of men, no anonymous majority of men, no distinguished aristocracy of men, no seminary of holy men is above the law of nature. I should go further than this. The law of nature does not of itself imply a religious view of life. But I am convinced that bodies of men will never in fact observe the law of nature over a period unless they accept the religious view. Of myself I know, and of others I believe, that no one can believe in the brotherhood of man and love his fellows unless he has seen his own utter worthlessness in the sight of a Universal Father and Creator of all and recognized his own inescapable duty to obey His law.

Of political conditions government by discussion is the only road to government by reason. Any short cut is ultimately a false move. Discussion is only possible in the four conditions named above, freedom of speech, autonomy of procedure, the widest publicity, and patriotism rising above party.

Finally, universal suffrage. This is an end as well as a means. Parliaments and all free institutions are born out of exclusive privilege, but develop by natural law into universal suffrage, or perish on the way. Western institutions have a respectable pedigree behind them, and they lead to this conclusion. In the matter of political equality there is no stopping at any half-way house.

On these conditions, is it possible to hope for the survival of Parliamentary institutions for mankind?

In order to answer this question I feel a comparison is necessary with other democratic and Parliamentary institutions on the British model. The omission of Continental and South American examples and of reference to the Soviet system is not the result either of contempt or dislike; it is simply that in a book on the British Parliament other Anglo-Saxon models afford on the whole a more fruitful comparison.

Comparisons, they say, are odious. And odious they are if their purpose is to compare the virtues of the things one holds dear oneself to the disadvantage of the things sacred in another man's eyes. All comparisons of this kind (and they are quite common) on both sides of the Atlantic between the American and British Constitution and customs, designed to show that one is better, or more just, or more efficient, or more democratic than the other, are misguided.

But there is another kind of comparison—the object of which is to promote understanding and good feeling. It is important for British people to try to understand how Americans feel about their Constitution, and for Americans to understand that all British people are quite as satisfied with their traditional Constitution as it has developed, as Americans are with their own written Constitution. And for both it is important to feel after a wider truth; neither Constitution is perfect. But each with all its faults is better and more suited to its own country than would be a hastily adapted version of the other.

For here is a great political truth. The "ideal State" of the philosophers is a myth and dream. True, what is and what ought to be are not one and the same thing. But God's providence designed men and peoples to be different. A perfect child of five and a perfect man of eighty would not be the same. The "I" that ought to be, is as different from the "you" that ought to be, as the "I" that is, differs from the "you" that is. People do not become more like one another as they become better.

In this, races and nations are like individuals. The desert dweller need not try to imitate the Cockney or the Eskimo. His laws and his customs need to be changed to conform to the will of the Creator, but they do not need to be denaturalized. They must remain his own, suited to the place in which he lives, and the kind of life that is suitable to him. The universality of the moral law is not the same thing as identity of custom or culture. The ideal Britain, the ideal France, the ideal Canada, the ideal Russia, should be as different as their actual counterparts.

Let us compare American and British Codes of law in this spirit. The most striking difference between U.S.A. and the United Kingdom is the size. Britain, which is three nations, is rather smaller than some single States in the Union of forty-eight States. Across the American Continent is further than from London to Cairo. The area of England, Scotland, Wales, the Isle of Man and the Channel Islands is under ninety thousand square miles. The area of the United States is over three and a half million square miles. Practically nowhere in the United Kingdom is much more than six hundred miles from Westminster. Six hundred miles from Washington means nothing in the United States.

You will tell me that when the United States were formed out of the thirteen original colonies this was not true. The colonies represented a small area on the Atlantic seaboard. This is not quite correct. As the United States expanded so has the speed of travel accelerated and the United States are not much larger now in terms of man hours of travel than they were at the time of the Declaration of Independence.

Difference in size explains in part the two basic differences in the two great democratic Constitutions of the world. America is naturally a federation. Britain is naturally a unitary sovereignty. If America were to be governed from a single centre in the same sense that Britain is governed from Westminster she would no longer be free. Differences of climate, development, outlook and interest are all too great to permit of centralization without loss of freedom. The individual rights of the forty-eight States to legislate for themselves, and the limitations restraining the Congress or the President from imposing from Washington a uniform legal code may be carried to extremes by American Conservatives, but nonetheless represent the Ark of the Covenant of American liberty. America is a Federal Union, or an autocracy. To Britons the very meaning of federation is obscure. Her freedom lies in the flexibility and omnipotence of the instrument—Parliament—which her people elect. Yet Britain represents almost the extreme size to which a free state can grow without federation. Let the United Kingdom attempt to include Ireland and long and bitter controversy will arise.

The next most obvious difference is in history. The British national communities, English, Scots, Welsh, Irish, Cornish, are traditional. They have grown up as communities. Our ancestors lived together as we live together ourselves. To us, therefore, law means custom and tradition. We place great reliance on conventional forms but manage to reconcile extreme flexibility of substance with almost uncanny rigidity of external observance. Moreover, we are interested in the status of individuals within the community rather than the opportunities for individuals regarded as such.

With the Americans the situation is reversed. An American whose ancestors were in the Continent before 1840 is an exception, and in the main they emigrated as individuals, not as communities.

When they arrived what they found would have been a hotch-potch of individuals, a melting-pot of humanity without traditions, without standards, without social form, but for what? But for precisely defined legal rights. A Constitution, a declaration of the rights of man, combined with the most rigid protection for the rugged individualism of the pioneer, a complete rejection in principle of everything that caste or privilege implies. We can afford to encourage and teach Welsh and Gaelic in our schools. Americans cannot afford to do other than insist so far as is possible that English is the language that American citizens must be brought up to speak. But for their language and their Constitution there would be no nation; the individual for them is everything. The Briton wraps himself in the immemorial antiquity of customary forms.

Another comparison. Until within living memory there was no time in American history when there was not a frontier—to which younger sons, adventurers, immigrants, failures, rolling stones of all sorts could resort in order to try their luck and found or restore their fortunes. There was no lack of virgin land for the occupation. A Briton who wanted to change his status fundamentally must emigrate. There was no frontier in our small island. But we founded an Empire.

Both America and Britain have been strategically secure and find it difficult to sympathize with the mentality of European peoples whose land has been overrun by an invading army twice in a generation. But in comparison with Britons, Americans are still more carefree. Once Britain had beaten Spain and France, there was no Power on earth which could threaten the United States except Britain herself with her command of the sea. This, the War of Independence, and the large number of Americans of Catholic and Irish descent explain an occasional bitterness of criticism against Britain in America which, so far from being reciprocated, is met with complete incomprehension here. Britain, on the other hand, although never invaded, always had a more complex system of security.

She could never afford to permit a power to gain control of the narrow seas, or a single power to dominate the Atlantic coast of Europe. Alliances, balances, negotiations, coalitions were the essence of British policy until the battle of Trafalgar gave her supremacy at sea for a century. This dream has been shattered by the air war. America, even in the atomic age, can still afford a degree of carelessness which even in the nineteenth century Britain could hardly achieve.

America is of course interested in overseas trade. But Britain cannot feed her population even on the barest necessities on what her own soil produces. Commerce, trade with foreign countries are her life-blood. There are few British families who have not a son, an uncle, or a brother in some quite remote parts of the earth. American families have their family ties with their country of origin. When these slacken the interest in the outside world is remote. Such internationalism as exists in the United States is therefore based on racial origin. In Britain it is based mainly on travel.

The American Constitution was founded at a time when the British Constitution had not truly developed its characteristic form. Britain was a monarchy indeed, and the temporary reaction to absolutism under George III made her seem more so than she was. The Royal Cabinet, Members of a corrupt House of Commons, dominating it by patronage and bribes, seemed an evil excrescence, not as we view it now a gradually emergent instrument to obey the people's will and serve its interests. The fathers of the American Constitution framed their own on the model most familiar to them. There must be a King, Lords and Commons. But the King must be elected, not hereditary, and although clothed with the real prerogatives of power he must not be hedged about with the almost divine aura of majesty; his prerogatives must be watched and controlled, and his term of office must be limited. Britons have never understood why Americans were so touchy about the Third Term. That is because they think of America as a Republic with the President as a sort of Prime Minister. It is not; it is a limited and elected monarchy held for the short period of four years at a time by a man with the powers of a king. Americans have never understood why we are as angry to hear the King or Queen spoken of with disrespect as we should be to hear ill spoken of our family. They roughly criticize their own President. That is because they think of this island as a monarchy ruled over by right of birth and not election, and for life and not a period. It is not; it is a republic with a hereditary President, who is clothed with majesty and pomp precisely because he is the beloved symbol of his people and their humble lives, and is stripped of real power precisely because he is so much beloved that he cannot be brought into controversy.

No one can fail to see the deliberate analogy of the Senate and the House of Lords. The Americans rationalized the House of Lords by making it elective and justified its existence by making it the corner-stone of States' rights.[1] Thus we can never understand how the Americans can tolerate a state of affairs where there is a perpetual bickering between two fully elective democratic assemblies embodying different electoral principles. The Americans can never understand how we can tolerate a Second Chamber with such wide theoretical powers, composed neither of elected members, nor of men who for the most part lay the least claim to be politically important.

We can never understand why it is possible for President and Congress to be of a different political flavour. The Americans do not comprehend why we do not fear an omnipotent Parliament. We do not see why the Americans exclude members of their Cabinet from Congress. Americans would regard their inclusion as subversive of the fundamentals of the Constitution.

The federal character of the American Constitution necessitates an institution which has no parallel here. If Congress itself is to be of limited power and the rights of states guarded against it, and if the President himself cannot arbitrate between them for fear of making him absolute, the American Supreme Court is a necessary consequence. No court in Britain can adjudicate on the legality of an Act of Parliament, although any superior court can and does decide whether local authorities, Ministers of the Crown, and even single Houses of Parliament are acting within their rights. No authority in the United States, neither President, Congress nor state legislature is immune from the jurisdiction of the Supreme Court.[2] The Supreme Court was in fact modelled on the colonial jurisdiction of the Privy Council which to this day sometimes decides the legality of Acts of the Canadian legislature.

This brings one to another fruitful and interesting scene of comparison—between the institutions of the United States, Britain, and the various British Dominions.

Canada has the size which demands a constitution on the federal model. That makes her constitution largely a revised model of the American. But hers was hived off at a moment after the

---

[1] The House of Representatives is elected on the basis of population, but the States are equally represented in the Senate whatever their population.

[2] Technically that is not quite true. The Supreme Court does not adjudicate on an Act of Congress, but simply decides that, since it was unconstitutional, it must be ignored in determining the rights of the parties.

full constitutional development of the Cabinet system had occurred. The principle of the Canadian Executive therefore follows the British rather than the American model. The Canadians have had to deal with a further problem of even greater complexity than the American problem of mixed immigration. Apart from immigrants the Canadians are of two distinct races of widely differing culture and tradition, separated geographically and not intermingled as in the United States, and comparable in size with one another, not like the numerically negligible French minority in Louisiana.

The French Canadians are traditionalist, Roman Catholic, French speaking. The British Canadians are Protestants conforming more than they like to believe to the American type. Canada is the meeting-point of three great spiritual forces—the American way of life, the British Commonwealth and the French Canadian. This fact fundamentally influences their institutions, and their policy in the present generation of Canadians has given rise to an intense spiritual ferment—barely concealed and held in check in the older generation by the bromide of political liberalism.

Australia has federal institutions, but no racial problem. The outcome is a typically English type of Constitution with modifications from the United States. New Zealand, two relatively small islands, has copied Britain almost exactly with a Second Chamber (but without the hereditary House of Lords). South Africa, another federation, has the most complicated racial and political problem in the world. The tension between British and Dutch is solved by a federal system (in which, however, the federal legislature is apparently able to alter the Constitution).[1] Racial problems between African and European, African and Indian, and Indian and European communities, not to speak of a definite if mild tendency to anti-semitism, are still to solve. Eire appears to have solved her Constitutional problems by giving herself a sovereign legislature based on proportional representation but with the outlook and general policy of a county council controlled by a Watch Committee of Roman Catholics. Her position is interesting mainly as that of a Dominion which claims to be an independent republic, an independent republic which none the less recognizes the King for certain external purposes, a member of the Commonwealth that yet remained neutral during the war, and a neutral which none the less supplied a greater proportion of fighting men

---

[1] This appears to have been decided by the Supreme Court in Ndlwana *v.* Hofmeyer.

to the British forces than certain parts of the Commonwealth. To such extent can history create paradoxes.

We have now taken a fairly rapid survey of Constitutions in Britain, the Dominions, and the United States. All are democratic. All have certain striking differences. How far are they or any of them articles of export, or how far are they of peculiar use only to the English-speaking Dutch and Scandinavian peoples?

The answer appears not to be an absolute "yes" or an absolute "no." There are certain conditions without which free and representative Parliamentary Government is impossible. First there must be a desire within the community for a single Government of the Parliamentary type. Communities too deeply divided by class, religion or race cannot enjoy free representative institutions. Thus the United Kingdom of Great Britain and Ireland has fallen apart, Jew and Arab seem unable to agree in Palestine, Moslem and Hindu in India, black and white in South Africa; Teuton and Slav in Czechoslovakia.

But given goodwill and given discreet use of the federal principle there seems no reason why these difficulties should not be overcome. In Switzerland, a country of only sixteen thousand square miles, but with a peculiar geography and a federal constitution, Roman Catholic and Protestant communities live side by side in perfect harmony, and German, French, Italian and Romansh peoples dwell in neighbouring valleys supporting common laws, and a single nationality. In Canada the same is true. In South Africa, British and Dutch succeed, but Europeans and Africans have not so far succeeded. India remains a problem to be solved. Perhaps it is more than a coincidence that the only successful examples of federation are in Christian countries.[1]

Second, there appear to be areas of the world in which geography prevents the growth of democracy. Parliamentary democracy would be as difficult to cultivate among the Bedouin as potatoes in the desert—yet they know a fraternity, liberty and equality of a kind in some ways not inferior. No one complains of the kindly Danish tutelage of Greenland, and although a demand for freedom exists no one doubts that even the European imperialism at its worst was a far preferable thing in Africa to uncontrolled exploitation by the whisky pedlar, the slave trader and the private adventurer.

---

[1] The Arab Federation is not a federal state.

Third, there seems to be a maximum size for free institutions and a minimum development of communications without which Parliamentary democracy will not work. The Soviet system is often criticized in this country. But how far are its differences the product of limited communications, incomplete industrialization, and enormous size? China has never really approximated to freedom; nor has Japan. No one knows whether India with four hundred million inhabitants, mostly illiterate, can coagulate into a single state even assuming the solution of the communal and caste problems, and the problem created by the princely states. Our own march towards Parliamentary democracy has been slow, and the result of material factors often as much as intellectual or moral excellence. Shall we assume that others will be much quicker?

In other States, such as Spain, Germany, Italy and France, political freedom has been spasmodic, and interrupted by periods of reaction. Was this due to the unsuitability of democracy even on European soil?

My answer is "no." The failure of democracy in France and the Latin countries was as much constitutional as temperamental. They failed to create institutions with an Executive sufficiently powerful to control the country; they were therefore cursed with periods in which powerful Executives governed without Constitutions. In Germany the failure was opposite. For a variety of reasons German nationalism failed to express itself in a legislature effective to control the already powerful traditional Executive based on an aristocracy in alliance with a powerful prince. The like would probably have happened here if the prince and the aristocracy had not indulged in mortal struggle. French, Russian, Italian and German emigrants make admirable Americans in a single generation; there is, therefore, nothing in the type incompatible with democracy.

I answer, therefore, that with reasonable allowances for differences in geography, culture and state of development, Parliamentary democracy, based on a Christian culture and fortified where necessary by federal institutions, is an article capable of an application practically universal within a reasonable time—capable of indefinite extension from generation to generation.

I have reached the end of my journey, but I ask one further question. Can the area be extended beyond the frontiers of nations so as to include the world?

CHAPTER XXIV

A World Parliament?

CAN there be a World Parliament? On November 22nd, 1945, speaking from the Front Opposition Bench, Mr. Eden spoke as follows:—

"Let me come to what seems to me to be the fundamentals of this problem. The truth is that by the discovery of this atomic energy science has placed us several laps ahead of every present phase of international political development, and unless we can catch up politically to the point we have reached in science, and thus command the power which at present threatens us we are all going to be blown to smithereens. I think that Mr. Byrnes put it quite well at Charleston when he said that the civilized world could not survive an atomic war, and I agree entirely with the Prime Minister that no set of rules will enable us to survive a future war when this weapon is latent to use.

"I agree too that no safeguards by themselves will provide an effective guarantee. They have to be accompanied by the rule of law amongst the nations. It is something more than one hundred years ago that Castlereagh first conceived the idea of making progress in diplomacy by contact. He was on the right line, but he failed. After the last war nations tried again by the League to make another effort more in conformity with the developments that had taken place in the intervening period, and they failed; and during this war we at San Francisco tried again, and have sought to lay the foundations of a new world order.

"The truth is that all the inventions of recent years have tended the same way, to narrow the world, and therefore to intensify the shock and sharpen the reaction before the shock absorbers are ready. Every succeeding scientific discovery makes greater nonsense of old-time conceptions of sovereignty, and yet it is not the least use deluding ourselves any more than Mr. Byrnes did in his Charleston speech. It is yet time that national sentiment is still strong as ever, and here and there it is strengthened by this further complication, the different conception of forms of government and . . . of words like freedom and democracy.

"So, despite some stirrings, the world has not so far been ready to abandon, or even really to modify, its old conceptions of sovereignty. But there have been some stirrings. There was the Briand plan after the last war for the federation of Europe. . . . In the darkest hour of 1940 there was the offer made to France by Mr. Churchill, and there were the various suggestions made between the U.S. and ourselves.

"Now atomic energy has come to enforce the call for something more, because the world family is smaller to-day than was the European family at the end of the last war. I have thought much on this question of atomic energy both before and since that bomb burst on Nagasaki, and for the life of me I have been unable to see any final solution which will make the world safe for atomic power, save that we all abate our present idea of sovereignty. . . .

"We have got somehow to take the sting out of nationalism. We cannot hope to do so at once, but . . . we should make up our minds where we want to go. . . . I know where I want to go. I want to get a world in which the relations between the nations can be transformed in a given period of time . . . as the relations between Scotland and Wales in this country have been transformed."

Mr. Eden is the acknowledged expert of the Conservative Party on Foreign Affairs, and there is probably no statesman alive in the world, even including Mr. Churchill and Marshal Stalin, so intimately acquainted as he with the details of world events in the last ten years.

Mr. Bevin who claimed to speak as an individual but not as a Foreign Secretary said in the same debate: "Often after 1940 I have tried to study how we could have given effect to Mr. Churchill's offer to France, and it seemed to me that joint citizenship involved joint parliament, and joint responsibility. It involved the acceptance of this for certain limited purposes in order to derive the powers of law.

"Therefore when you turn from all the things you have built up—your League of Nations or your Constitution[1]—I feel we are driven relentlessly along this road. We need a new study for the purpose of creating a world assembly elected directly from the people of the world as a whole to whom the Governments who form the United Nations are responsible, and who, in fact, make the world law which they, the people will then accept and be morally bound and willing to carry out. . . .

[1] Sc. of U.N.O.?

"The supreme art of Government is the horrible duty of deciding matters which affect the life or death of the people. That power rests in the House so far as this country is concerned. I would merge that power into the greater power of a directly elected world assembly in order that the great repositories of destruction and science, on the one hand, may be their property, against the misuse of which it is their duty to protect us, and on the other hand that they may determine whether a country is acting as an aggressor or not.

"I am willing to sit with anybody, of any party of any nation, to try to devise a franchise or a constitution . . . for a world assembly . . . for a limited objective—the objective of peace. Once we can get to that stage, I believe we shall have taken a great progressive step."

If language has any meaning, this exchange of views cannot be disregarded at the conclusion of this book. Here are the two spokesmen of the two parties proposing in different language the same thing as the objective of foreign policy in this country. And the thing which they propose is nothing less than the subjection of our Parliament to a Parliament of the World—the Federation of Mankind.

Why? Each has been impressed by the destructive power of modern war. It is not that another war will destroy civilization. That, oddly enough, war cannot do, unless someone were unlucky enough to blow up the whole planet by mistake. Destructive agents, even the atomic bomb, always leave a certain number of people behind who can make and control the destructive agency; material civilization therefore survives in a sense, and the human values are not destroyed by atomic, or other bombs.

No. But what is true is this. Another war will probably mean that the atomic bomb will be used, and it will go on being used until there is only one set of men in charge of the only remaining means of making the atomic bomb.

New weapons do not destroy civilization; but they do destroy forms of government and radically alter the structure of human society.

Given only the apparatus at present in existence the material means for world government are already known and will be used until world government is a fact.

World Government is inevitable; the only uncertain factors are within what period of time and in what form. The choice is not between world government and no world government, or between world government and chaos. The choice is whether we have a free world government or an unfree world government. The task before democratic statesmen is to set up the standard of free world government in an acceptable form as soon as possible.

How? Is the Charter of the United Nations Organization enough? Quite obviously not. Why? Because though it is free it does not make for world government. A Government implies a legislature to make the law, and Executive to enforce it, a Court to apply it. The United Nations Organization is only a perpetual Peace Conference in which each great power has the right of veto.

Mr. Eden said within a month or two of the signature of the Charter with such pomp and ceremony: "The Charter is an anachronism in the modern world." I think he meant just what he said. The Charter is not wicked, or foolish or wrong. It is an anachronism, and it will ultimately be replaced by world government—though not necessarily by free world government.

What are the essentials of a free World Government? Clearly a Parliament, an Executive, and a Court.

Clearly, too, the Parliament must be federal, that is, limited in power; and clearly too, it must be open to the Court to question its decisions. Clearly also, therefore, the Court must not be nominated by the Parliament.

How is the Parliament to be elected? Mr. Eden was right when he said that never was national feeling so strong. Clearly a happy world is made up of happy nations, as happy nations are made up of happy families and local communities, not just a mere set of disconsolate individuals. The representatives must therefore be the representatives of free peoples.

But who is to vote and how? Mr. Bevin said that the assembly should be directly elected, apparently over the heads of the national governments, by the people of the world. Did he really mean this, and if so, what is to be the basis of the franchise? Does Mr. Bevin propose one man, one vote? There are four hundred and fifty millions of Chinese, one hundred and fifty millions each of Americans and Russians, forty-seven millions in this island, about three million Norwegians, and about a million and a half New Zealanders. Clearly this will not do. Then shall we have one country, one vote? That would mean Switzerland, Paraguay and South Africa would count for as much as U.S.A., Great Britain and Russia. Clearly this would not do. Some have suggested taxable capacity as the basis. This would bring America, Britain and Russia to the top and would correspond with the tentative arrangements for the Fund and the Bank agreed at Bretton Woods. But would the world accept a plutocracy as the basis of their new free democracy? Perhaps they would have to. After all, Parliament was plutocratic long before it developed into a democracy.

Would the nations accept election of representatives over the heads of the Governments? Quite clearly not—but this does not quite dispose of Mr. Bevin's suggestion of an assembly directly elected. The elections, though free, would be worked through the existing national machinery and would yield results which must differ according to the nature of the régime. But it is not clear that such a principle is more attractive than the present method of representation by governments.

Who would be the executive? As in all political arrangements the Executive would, in fact, be those who possessed the power, and those carrying the real responsibility. Not satisfactory? No— but the important thing is to make those with power amenable to law not of their making, not to deprive them of power—an end usually unattainable, and always unattainable without a struggle. Democracy was founded on much experience of constitutions not perfectly democratic.

What should be the Court? Clearly the Court is the protector of minorities, the defender of the principle of individual sovereignty under a régime which abates it, therefore representative mainly of the weak rather than the strong. Clearly it must consist of judges appointed for life, not paid by their own nation, and irremovable except for personal misconduct. Can we find any such who can be trusted? Have we tried?

Is there any sign of the possibility of such an outcome? Even the inevitable happens far more slowly than they believe who have seen its approach. The time scale of the Creator does not, to our infinite disappointment, coincide with the expectations of those whose span is threescore years and ten. Men said that the Reform Bill of 1832 was a revolution. So it was; but the consequences which they foresaw did not fully accomplish themselves for a century.

So we do not say that there will be no more wars. We do not say that if there be another war humanity will perish utterly. That men said in 1919. What we do say is something distinct, in a sense more portentous. For the first time in the history of the planet men are in possession of material equipment which given no improvement in outlook or political technique will yet make world government of some sort inevitable sooner or later, and which until it achieves this will make lasting peace on earth impossible even for men of goodwill. In Mr. Eden's phrase, our political equipment must catch up with our scientific attainments. Whether it will be free government or not depends upon those who believe in free government. That it will be modelled on existing institutions of some sort whether free or unfree no student of history can doubt, and that if free it must be modelled on an extension of Parliamentary and federal institutions as known and perfected in Britain and America also goes without saying, since there is no alternative from which it is reasonable to choose. Nonetheless it may be centuries and must be generations before the process is complete or even before the decisive step is taken.

One last question. Are we attempting the impossible? Can such an ambitious project ever achieve success? The Tower of Babel is something more than a myth. It is allegory. To break down the limitations of sovereignty, to overcome the divisions of language, to abolish war from the face of the earth, are these within the compass of human political genius? Or are they not contrary to the whole conditions of human existence whereby man was born to trouble as the sparks fly upward?

According to the legend, the Tower of Babel failed, not because what was attempted was imprudent or wicked, nor because in itself, it was impossible of attainment. Failure lay in the fact that its constructions were built in confidence in the possibilities of purely human achievement undertaken for purely human motives. There are spiritual conditions of success as well as political. I do not believe that the ultimate fate of man upon this planet can be divorced from his spirituality, and I do not believe that his spirituality can be divorced from his conscious attitude to the religion of the Bible. The story of the Old Testament is the story of constant rebellion against a code which was known but departed from because its observance was found to be irksome. The story of these last two thousand years is of constant rebellion against the truth of a revelation which is as yet imperfectly understood and which none the less has made constant advances or retreated only to resume its progress. Yet of this I am certain. The institutions of men can only achieve blessing if they consciously seek it. Except the Lord build the house, they labour in vain that build it. Except the Lord keep the city, the watchman watcheth but in vain.

INDEX

ABDICATION, 18, 19, 54.

Absentee voter, 35.

Acts of Parliament, 28, 167; Annual Army, 148; Appropriation, 146, 147; Consolidated Fund, 146, 147; Education, 56; Emergency Powers, 148, 149; Finance, 146, 147; Government of Ireland, 42; Ministers of the Crown, 63; National Health Insurance, 165; Naval Discipline, 148; Parliament (1911), 28, 29, 131, 171; Parliament Act Procedure, 139; Septennial, 131; of Settlement, 5. *See also Bills.*

Address, forms of, 121; method of, 120.

Adjournment, 128, 148, 165 *(see also Chapter XVIII);* daily half-hour, 174.

Administration, 60, 69, 70, 80, 126, 147, 151. *See also Chapter XII.*

Agent, 109.

Air raids, 142, 174.

Altar, 9.

Amendment, 140.

American Constitution, 17, 19, 53, 54, 62, 65, 67, 81, 85, 95, 109, 115, 153, 155, 177, 178, 179, 180.

American Fathers, 67.

American Loan, 142.

Amery, L. C. M. S., 19.

Anne, Queen, 5, 65.

Announcements, 129.

Answer. *See Question.*

Appeal, 68.

Appointments, 60.

Arundell, Archbishop, 47.

Asquith, H. H., 165.

Athenian policy, 58, 75, 76.

Atomic energy, 185, 186, 187.

Attorney General, 60, 62.

Auditor General, 146, 148.

Australia, 182.

BALFOUR, First Earl of, 145.

Ballot, 35; box, 114.

Barons, 5.

Barry, Sir Charles, 11, 105.

B.B.C. *(see Broadcasting).*

Belgium, 89.

Benches, 119.

Bentham, Jeremy, 98.

Bevin, Ernest, 186.

Bills, 117, 120, 122, 123, 146, 172; Money, 13, 27, 28, 146; Amendment of, 134, 136, 137, 139. *See Acts; also Chapter XVII.*

Birkenhead, Lord, 70.

Bishops, 23, 26, 27.

Bismarck, Prince, 94.

Blackstone, Sir William, 58.

Borough, 33, 35, 36, 37; franchise, 35, 36; "rotten," 36; "pocket," 36; "potwalloper," 36.

Boundaries, 42.

Boxes, red and green, 69.

Bracton, Henry de, 56.

Bradlaugh, Chas., 50.

Bretton Woods, 189.

Broadcasting, 103, 113.

Brown, W. J., 93, 96.

Budget, 28, 69, 146.

Buildings, 4, 92.

Burgesses, 33, 35.

Burke, Edmund, 43, 45, 81.

Business Question, 129.

Byrnes, James, 185.

CABINET, 16, 54, 55, 87, 144, 152, 153, 168, 176; list of ministers, 63. *See also Chapter IX.*

Cabinet Government, 6, 19, 69.

Campbell Case, 60.

Canada, 182.

Candidate, 154. *See also Chapter XIV.*

Canning, George, 86.

Card system, 77.

Cavaliers, 74.

Central Convention, 77.

Chair, 118.

Chamber, rebuilding of, 7.

Chamber of Deputies, 54.

Chamberlain, Joseph, 77.

Chamberlain, Neville, 72.

Chancellor of the Exchequer, 61, 62, 146.

Charles I, 35, 48, 68.

Charles II, 8, 27, 35, 74, 148.
Church, 5.
Churchill, Lord Randolph, 89.
Churchill, Winston, 7, 72, 84, 157, 172.
Civil Service, 6, 69, 70, 80, 126. *See also Chapter XII.*
Civil War, 48, 76, 100.
Clause. *See Bill.*
Clergy, 8, 33.
Clerk, to the House of Commons, 119, 139; to the Table, 125, 126.
Coalition, 65, 66, 83, 115, 167.
Cobbett, William, 102.
Colonies, 20.
Commission under the Great Seal, 16, 139, 140, 171.
Committee(s), 11, 134; stage, 136, 166; system, 70, 153; rooms, 13; of: Ways and Means, 28, 146; Supply, 28, 146; Privileges, 68; Public Accounts, 68, 148; Scrutinising, 68; Imperial Defence, 71; Standing, 135; Scottish, 135; Select, 62, 65, 132, 148, 167; The whole House, 135, 146.
Commons, 8, 28, 29, 68, 133, 144, 145. *See also Chapter V.*
Comptroller, 146, 148.
Congress, 19, 53, 54, 65, 81, 85, 181.
Conservatism, 55.
Conservative Party, 76, 78, 79, 145.
Constituencies, 54, 55; nursing of, 108. *See also Chapter XIV.*
Constituents, 14, 147.
Constitution, 2, 17, 53, 54, 63, 65, 67, 75, 87, 144, 149, 169. *See also Chapter XXIII.*
Contempt, 49.
Continental Democracies, 54, 76, 90.
Conversational style, 8.
Convocations, 8, 26, 33.
Conway, General, 48.
Co-operative Societies, 77.
Coronation Oath, 17.
Correspondents. *See Press.*
Council of Greater Barons, 34.
Councillors of the King, 27.
Counsel, 132.
County Councils, 33.
County franchise, 34, 35.
Court of Requests, 9.
Criminal offences, 60.
Criticism, 89, 90, 168, 169.

Cromwell, Oliver, 148.
Cross Benches, 9.
Crossing the floor, 7.
Crown, 5, 17, 49, 54, 61, 66, 68, 69, 99, 130, 140, 142, 144, 146, 147, 166; expenditure of, 147.
Crown of Confessor, 17.
Crown Lands, 4, 147.
Curzon, Lord, 70.
Custom, 8.

DEBATE, 27, 55, 104, 117, 134, 162; on the address, 140, 146. *See also Adjournment.*
Delegation, 165. *See also Chapter XX.*
Democracy, 58, 81, 88, 90, 109, 115, 144, 168. *See also Chapter XXIII.*
Departments, 70, 126, 147; list of, 150.
Despotism, 3.
Diaries, 100.
Dictatorship, 58, 87.
Discipline, 79, 82, 99.
Discussion, curtailment of. *See Chapter XXI.*
Disraeli, Benjamin, 66, 82, 105, 145, 157, 162.
Dissolution, 54, 68, 146.
Divisions, 79, 123; list, 123.
Doctrine of Mandate, 58.
Dominions, 182.
Draft, 133.

EDEN, Anthony, 185, 188.
Edward I, 5, 9, 32, 33, 34, 35.
Edward III, 35.
Edward VI, 117.
Edward VII, 19.
Egbert, 17.
Eire, 90, 182.
Election, 32, 37, 83; campaign, 110. *See also Chapters VI and XIV.*
Electoral Reform, 76.
Electorate, 68, 82, 83, 144.
Eleven o'clock Rule, 142, 164, 174.
Elizabeth, Queen, 5, 74, 99, 105, 133; Lord Keeper, 47.
Estimates, 146, 147, 148.
Executive. *See Cabinet.*
Exempted Business, 142, 174.
Expenditure, 69, 146, 147, 153.

Expenses, of Candidates, 109; of Members (*see Chapter XX*).
Explanations, personal, 129.
Expulsions, 50, 79.

FAGGOT voter, 35.
Federal principle, 40, 183, 186.
Feudal Policy, 8.
Finance, procedure of, 5, 69. *See Expenditure, and Bills* (*Money*).
Fires, 9.
Folders, 126.
Foreign Office Telegrams, 69.
Foreign Policy, 61.
Franchise, 32, 33, 34, 35, 37, 94.
French Chamber of Deputies, 68.
French Constitution, 85.
Front Bench, 78.

GALLERY, Civil Servants', 92; Press, 101; Visitors', 105; Ladies', 105; Speaker's Friends', 105; Peers', 105. *See also Chapter XIII.*
General Election, 108, 171.
George I, 5.
George III, 19, 78.
George V, 18, 19.
German aircraft, 9.
Gladstone, W. E., 6, 145, 163, 165.
Gordon, S., 157.
Government, 88, 115, 134, 143, 144, 148, 162, 172; forms of, 182, 183, 184; constitutional, 24; by force, 2; by discussion, 2, 3, 58, 88, 99, 115, 152, 162, 175, 176.
Great Councils, 24, 32.
Great Purse, 23.
Green card, 14.
Grievances, 141, 147.
Group System, 7.

HANOVERIAN Succession, 19, 61.
Hansard, 48, 101, 102, 123, 128.
Haxey Case, 47.
Henry II, 32, 33.
Henry III, 5, 34.
Henry IV, 27.
Henry V, 130.
Henry VI, 130.
Henry VII, 117.

Henry VIII, 9, 35, 37.
History of England, 74.
Hitler, 56, 61.
Hoare-Laval Pact, 144.
Hobhouse (Lord Broughton), 86.
Holland, 89.
Home Rule, 145.
Home Secretary, 60, 149.
Honourable, right, 121; and learned, 121; and gallant, 121; gentleman, 121; friend, 121.
Honours, 60.
Hooker, R., 99.
House of Representatives, 19, 62, 115.
Humble Address. *See Chapter XVIII.*
Hybrid Bill. *See Bill.*

IMPEACHMENT, 48.
Imposts, 69.
Independent Labour Party, 77.
Institutions, 82.
Invasion, immunity from, 1.
Irish, 163, 164; Treaty, 26, 42.

JAMES I, 5, 27, 48, 99, 135.
Japan, 1, 61.
John, King, 5, 34.
Johnson, Dr., 101.
Journals, 99.
Justice, 60.

"KEEP doors," 80.
Keys, of boxes, 69.
King, 4, 5, 6, 50, 56, 57, 61, 62, 130, 139, 140, 171; displeasure of, 47.
"King's Friends," 78. *See also Chapter III.*
King's Speech, 140, 146, 148.
Knights, 33.

LABOUR Government, 135, 149; Ministers of, 63, 166.
Labour Party, 77, 79, 91.
Labour Representation Committee, 77.
Language, unparliamentary, 121.
Laski, Professor, 25, 31.
Laws, 56; of inheritance, 25; of Nature, 57, 176.

Law Lords, 23, 26.
Legislation, 151, 162, 166; delegation of, 166, 167.
Letters, 12, 173, 174.
Letters Patent, 25.
Libel, 47.
Liberal Government, 6, 29, 145.
Licensing Laws, 50.
Lloyd George, David, 71.
Lobbies, 123.
Local Association, 76.
Local Authorities, 152.
Logic, 8.
Long Parliament, 117.
Lord Chancellor, 22, 23, 27, 60, 63.
Lord President of Council, 62.
Lord Privy Seal, 62.
Lords, 8, 9, 10, 109, 131, 134, 138, 149, 163, 174, 181. *See also Chapter IV.*
Lords Spiritual, 23.
Louis XIV, 18.
Loyalty, of ministers, 66.

MACAULAY, Lord, 74, 75.
Mace, 23, 118.
Magna Carta, 4, 25, 32.
"Maiden" Speech, 121.
Manual of Procedure, 68, 122.
Marvell, Andrew, 100.
Members, 12, 13, 14, 15, 62, 99, 103, 105, 120, 124, 126, 136, 141, 143, 154, 173; payment of, 37. *See also Chapter VI.*
Mercy, 60.
Microphone, 104.
Ministers, 23, 94, 126, 166, 173. *See also Chapter IX.*
Model Parliament, 32, 34, 35, 36.
Modern Parliament, 6.
Monarchy, 19.
Montfort, Simon de, 33.
Morrison, Herbert, 167.
Muir, Ramsay, 31.
Multi Party System, 85.

NATIONAL Liberal Federation, 77.
National Party Conference, 77.
National Union of Conservatives, 77.
Nationalism, 186.
Nationalization, 151.
New Zealand, 104, 182.
"Noble," 121.

Nomination, 108; papers of, 109.
Norman Conquest, 4, 18.
Norman Kings, 24.

OAKS, 11.
Oath, of secrecy, 61; of allegiance, 89; of supremacy, 105.
Office of Profit under Crown, 44.
Official Reports. *See Hansard.*
Opposition, 148, 168, 176; Leader of, 85; Bench, 86. *See also Chapter XI.*
Orders in Council, 166.
Order Papers, 126, 127, 128, 143.
Oxford, Parliament at, 8.

PALACE of Westminster, 9.
Palmerston, Lord, 162.
Parliament, perfection of, 3; physical structure of, 4, 7, 8, 10, 92; periods of, 5.
Parties, 88-91. *See also Chapter X.*
Party, Agent, 77; Association, 107, 109; Executive Committee, 108; Fund, 76; Organization, 76; System, 6, 54, 68, 89, 144, 149; organizations of, 6. *See also Chapter X.*
Patronage Secretary, 78.
Peel, R., 19, 76, 145, 163.
Peerage, 25, 62.
Peers, 54. *See Chapter IV.*
Pepys, Samuel, 93.
Petition, 117, 130, 133.
Pink Slips, 14.
Places, position in House, 119.
Policy, 2, 81, 88, 95, 96, 98, 114, 144; feudal, 8; adjustment of, 2; announcements of, 129.
Poll, 114, 145.
Popular will, 58.
Posters, 112.
Powers of Parliament, 67, 68. *See also Chapter VIII.*
P.P.S., 92.
Prayer, 9; right of, 166.
Preamble. *See Bill.*
President of U.S.A. *See American Constitution.*
Press, 48, 75. *See also Chapter XIII.*
Prime Minister, 21, 59, 60, 62, 67, 72.
Prints, Coffee House, 100.

Private, Bill (*see Bill*); Business, 127; Member, 124, 134, 141, 147, 163.

Privileges, of Parliament, 118, 129; breach of, 100. *See also Chapter VII.*

Privy Council, 16, 89.

Privy Councillors, 23, 61.

Proceedings, publication of, 100.

Procedure, 5, 147, 154 (*see also Chapters XV, XVI and XVII*); in Lords, 23; reforms in, 6, 164; in Bills (*see Chapter XVII*); in Money Bills, 146, 147, 148; in Committee (*see Chapter XVII*).

Proclamation, 16, 20, 26, 54, 55, 108, 171.

Propaganda, 113.

Proportional representation, 41, 114.

Prorogation, 172.

Public, 98, 143; Bill (*see Bill*); funds, 146; Officials, 93; opinion, 56; services, 152.

Publicity. *See Chapter XIII.*

Punchayat, 60.

Punishment, of Members, 49, 50.

Purse, control of, 146.

QUESTION, putting of, 122. *See also Chapter XVI.*

RADICAL Party, 76.

Rallies, 108.

Readings, First, Second, and Third. *See Bill.*

Recess, 141, 172.

Reeve, 33.

Reformation, 26.

Reform Bill, 5, 28, 29, 35, 76, 77, 81.

Reforms: of Civil Service, 94, 164; of Lords, 30.

Reichstag, 82, 168.

Rejection, of Bill, 135.

Religion, 54, 74, 190.

Report Stage. *See Bill.*

Representative Principle, 5, 32, 33.

Resignation, 66, 68.

Resolutions, 172; of money, 146; of censure, 143. (*See also Chapter XVIII*).

Restoration, 100.

Richard II, 27.

Rights, Bill of, 47.

Roman Republic, 76.

Ross, J. F. S., 156.

Rostrum, 8.

Roundheads, 74.

Royal, Assent, 16, 55, 130, 131, 139; Charter, 35; Prerogative, 16, 20, 29, 54, 142, 166, 171; Proclamation (*see Proclamation*); Rejection, 16, 130, 131.

Royalty, symbolism of, 21.

Rules. *See Procedure.*

Russia, 87.

ST. STEPHEN's Chapel, 9, 105, 117; Hall, 9.

Salaries, 38, 42, 43, 63. *See also Chapter XX.*

San Francisco, 185.

Scandinavia, 89.

Schedules, 166. *See also Bill.*

Schnadhorst, 77.

Seats, 38; Northern Irish, 40, 42; University, 40, 41.

Secretaries of State, 62.

Sedition, 47.

Selection Committee, 107.

Senate, 62, 115, 181.

Separation of Powers, doctrine of, 65.

Sergeant-at-Arms, 119.

Sessions, 171; Secret, 49, 99, 105, 106.

Side Benches, 9.

Sittings, 172.

Shadow Cabinet, 85.

Shire Moots, 33; voting at, 34.

Slander, 47.

Smith, Sir Thomas, 52, 119, 120, 121, 122, 123, 133.

Snell, Lord, 44, 157.

Somerset, Lord Granville, 76.

South Africa, 182.

Sovereign. *See King.*

Sovereignty, Parliamentary, 53.

Speaker, 9, 16, 27, 117, 118, 119, 120, 123, 127, 129, 135, 140, 141; eye of, 104, 120; warrant of, 108; panel of, 136.

Speech, freedom of, 47, 48, 54, 148.

"Spoils" System, 95.

Statutes, 130.

Statutory Rules and Orders, 166.

Stuarts, 18, 105.

Strangers, withdrawal of, 105, 106.
Structure. *See Chapter XX.*
Subsidies, 27.
Suffrage, 40, 54, 55, 176.
Summons, 24, 32.
Supreme Court of Appeal, 26.
Suspension, 50.
Sword, control of, 146.

TABLE of the House, 118, 119, 166.
Taxes, 28, 33, 61, 69, 146, 147.
Team, 89, 115, 144.
Tellers, 123.
Ten Commandments, 57.
Third Republic, 67, 84.
Throne, 9.
Thucydides, 58.
Tickets, 105.
Timetable, 6, 68, 152. *See also Chapters XXI and XXII.*
Title. *See Bill.*
Tories, 74.
Township, 33.
Trade Unions, 77, 78, 95.
Trafalgar, Battle of, 180.
Treaty, 142; of Utrecht, 29.
Tudor Monarchy, 5, 18, 35.
Two-Party System, 76.

USUAL Channels. *See Whips.*
Underlining, 80.
Unemployment Regulations, 145.

United Nations Organization, 186; Charter of, 188.
Universal Suffrage, 115.

VACANCY, 108.
Verbatim Report. *See Hansard.*
Victoria, Queen, 19, 139.
Vote, 40, 144; university, 41; business, 40; at early elections, 34, 35; restriction, of, 34; of confidence, 144; floating, 55, 84, 91; casting, 118; taking of, 122, 123.
Voters, 77.

WADE, Dr., 56.
Walpole, Sir Robert, 173.
War, 151; Cabinet, 71; Council, 71; of Independence, 179; of Roses, 35; World War I, 71, 166—Cabinet of, 72; World War II, 72, 73, 166, 174—Cabinet of, 72.
Ward system, 77.
Westminster, 51; Abbey, 9, 117.
Whigs, 19, 74.
Whips, 78, 79, 80, 129, 141; written, 79.
Whitehall, 9.
William II, 65.
William III, 19, 48, 67.
Wireless. *See Broadcasting.*
Witan, 24.
Witnesses, 132.
Wolsey, Cardinal, 9.
Woolsack, 9, 23.
World Parliament, 154. *See also Chapter XXIV.*